THE COMMODITY OF
CONNECTION

How Authentic
Relationships
Saved My Life...

When
My Daughter
Lost Hers

MOLLY BICE-JACKSON

THE COMMODITY OF CONNECTION
How Authentic Relationships Saved My Life
When My Daughter Lost Hers

To request permissions, contact the publisher at publish@joapublishing.com.

Hardcover ISBN: 978-1-961098-94-7
Paperback ISBN: 978-1-961098-93-0
eBook ISBN: 978-1-961098-95-4
Printed in the USA.

Joan of Arc Publishing
Meridian, ID 83646
www.joapublishing.com

✦ Enjoy Exclusive Bonuses! ✦

Thank you for reading
The Commodity of Connection!
As a special thank you,
I've created exclusive bonuses just for you.

HOW TO ACCESS YOUR BOOK BONUSES

Simply scan the QR code below with your phone to
unlock your special resources:

Dedication

To my parents, Russell and Nancy Bice, who never stopped believing in me, loving me, and supporting me in all the ways, who held me in my grief while facing their own.

To Victor Michael Jackson, my partner in crime, my Vicky Poo, my Victor Schmictor Der Lichtor, my comaker of small humans, my rock, my roll, and the acceptor of my soul.

To my siblings: Amy, Nathan, and Taylor. They've seen me at my lowest, my weirdest, my ugliest, and smelled me at my stinkiest. And they still love me. We are lucky to have each other and to each be entirely fabulous as well as the funniest of people.

The mindset and heartset it took to bring forth these words were aided greatly by my guardian angels: my daughter Lucy, my dearest friend Justin Kinnaird, my cheerleader Jodi Roma, and my Grandma Gayle. This book is also dedicated to them.

To my loyal Instagram friends and followers who have witnessed my descent into madness and back many times and loved me regardless. (Yes, I'm talking to YOU. You know who you are.) Thank you for supporting me, believing in me, and waiting patiently for me to get this book into the world. I knew we could do it.

This book was championed beyond belief by my stellar friends Jessica Baker, Rachael Rawson Gull, Kerri Jones, Kelley Wolf, Eden Morris, Thea Greaves, Monica Gomez, Heather Mannson, Megan Helgason, Ty Bennett, Candace Burch, Emily Kennard Dunn, Kim Nelson Hirt, Amy Hackworth, Crocky, Jeffrey Scott Stevens, Sarah Peterson Whitmore, Chad Hardy, my entire Showtime Company family, Young Ambassadors family, MDT family, Kimball Ward family, Jackson Family, and my fellow MHS class of '96 besties.

A heartfelt dedication goes out to Primary Children's Hospital, the Park City Fire District, Utah Donor Connect, and Summit County Search and Rescue.

Until Keira Brinton and JOA Publishing, this book was a constant thorn lodged beneath my skin—always there, pulsing with discomfort, demanding attention, yet impossible to fully remove until the work was done. It throbbed, distracting me from everything else, but only through patient care and perseverance could it finally be eased. I owe this healing entirely to Keira for taking a chance on me after seeing one of my crazy, comedic Instagram posts.

Perhaps most importantly, this book is dedicated to and made possible by the dazzling duo–Zoloft and Adderall.

Oh! And we can't forget to dedicate this to and thank my children, Peter and Zoë, for "letting me" use my own damn laptop computer ON OCCASION so I could write.

TABLE OF CONTENTS

Preface

Most people believe that when you lose a child, you will never move on. They are correct. You won't. You will never move on as your old self because you will never be that person again. You'll be painfully reconfigured into a foreign shape you didn't know existed. Strangely enough, you *will* feel joy again. The hopelessness will end. And above all else, you will be violently, brilliantly awakened to the unfortunate and unrelenting complexity of what it means to be human.

I often think about the people who received my daughter's organs. I think about the visceral and very raw procedure that it takes to transplant an organ—both to harvest it and to receive it. Not until I began writing this book did it dawn on me that I was similarly cut open and required a new heart to be able survive: the mental and emotional transformation I went through was parallel to what those strangers out in the world experienced after receiving Lucy's liver and kidneys; the transition period, the acclamation, the monitoring of vitals (is Molly eating? sleeping? how's her blood pressure? is she taking her meds?) is similar. We cannot be left alone when new and foreign parts are introduced to our bodies, brains, and spirits. We need other capable humans to help us survive and heal.

Everyone has a BIG GRIEF. Maybe you haven't lost a child, but you've had your heart wrenched and experienced your own set of losses. I'm sorry to be the bearer of bad news, but there is more to come. You will need authentic connection to make it through.

The need for healing through connection isn't just for the "heart transplants," it's also for the hangnails, scrapes, bruises, stubbed toes, job losses, acne, loneliness, and paper cuts of life.

Connection isn't just for healing either. It is key for strength and resilience. If we want to be effective leaders, present parents, powerful friends, loving partners, and successful humans, we need to make connection a top priority.

This book is me not leaving you alone in your grief.

This book is your guide for acclimating you to your new life.

This book is me watching over you as you question whether or not you can go on living. This book is me taking you by the hand, looking you in the eyes—into the nightmares that have entered your life—and promising you that you'll survive this. This book is me encouraging you to take another step, get your butt out of bed, and try one more time. You can love, forgive, keep working toward that goal, and deal with that difficult client. You can. Despite what you think, your scars are beautiful and they can help you attain more of the greatest commodity on earth.

Also, this book is me absolutely shouting at you a million times that connection is everything. It saved my life when my daughter lost hers.

Introduction

You might be shocked at how many times I've sat down to write this book. You'd be equally amazed at the creative and persistent self-sabotage I've conjured up to keep my butt out of this chair. Some of you would laugh yourself silly if you knew just how much content I've already created over years of blogging, speaking, and journaling, yet how completely incapable I've been of organizing it all. It feels like trying to trap a wild animal in a cage, and frankly, I'm not equipped for that. In fact, if you follow me on social media or know me in real life, you know I have *zero* animal skills (which we can talk about later, if you'd like).

Between my ADD, imposter syndrome, chronic motherhood (one of the most debilitating conditions a human can live with), and a pandemic, the fact that you're reading these words on a printed page is nothing short of a modern-day miracle. If you don't believe in miracles, you should now. Consider every word in this book proof that miracles are real.

This is the fourth introduction I've written for this book, but it's the first one I'm not overthinking. I'm sitting at my kitchen table with puzzle pieces scattered around my laptop (turns out my pandemic brain really digs puzzles). My son is watching YouTube videos of a teenager in the UK playing Minecraft (why?!), and my daughter is running around the backyard in our dried-up pond with her friend.

She'll be inside in exactly 94 seconds to complain about the neighbor boys.

I don't care if anyone reads this. I don't care if I sell a million copies or make a million dollars—or $400, for that matter. I just need the voice in the back of my head to *shut up about it already*. I'm writing the damn book, so let me be!

My old publisher told me I needed to build my Instagram following. My insecurities keep whispering that I'm not qualified to write this book. My house constantly reminds me I don't have time to write this book because . . . laundry and dishes. And my computer? It's rebelling too, randomly hopping to different lines while I type. I might lose my mind.

But here's the truth: I don't care anymore. I don't have the energy to care. This is my story. This is my heart. This is my research. This is my calling.

This is my book.

I had an entire outline of this book completed—chapter titles, bullet points, fully written sections —and sent to my agent almost two years ago. Then, my computer died a miserable death, and I had nothing backed up. Guess what? I don't have that agent anymore either. I think he saw my Instagram antics and called it quits. I was too much for him. (Not to worry—the universe led me to the perfect publisher for Little Miss Molly!)

And I don't know why the gods whispered in my ear to sit down this random Wednesday afternoon in May and just *go for it* without overthinking or caring about anything, but they did.

And just like clockwork, my daughter has come inside to tell me Will and Evan are playing unfairly. Called it.

I can't hold this book in any longer. I know too many people who feel they'll never be able to fully live again after tragedy, heartache, or loss. Too many believe the only way out of their grief is to end their life. They've been dragged under by the unrelenting current of pain and trauma, and they're ready to drown.

If you're reading this while feeling like you're drowning, picture me floating toward you on a giant pink flamingo pool floatie. Not only do I want to show you that connection with others can rescue you, but we're going to have some fun in the process. Life can be a different ride. The currents and storms are still unpredictable, but with the right tools, you'll find your way through.

I once read, "There is someone out there with a wound in the exact shape of your words." —Sean Thomas Dougherty (from "Why Bother?" a poem in *The Second O of Sorrow: American Poets Continuum Series, 165*)

If your wound matches my words, let them be the healing balm they're meant to be. Let these words remind you that you're not alone. You're stronger than you think. Being human is hard, but you have permission to feel joy, even in the midst of being human—sometimes *because* of it. There is reason to hope.

Your ship might be sinking, your heart might be shattered, your company might be struggling—just hold on. I'm here to connect with you. We all have a story of our rise and our fall. The question is, do we have the faith to get still enough to hear and answer the call?

In my case, the call I heard—and chose to embrace—centers around the power of connection. Connection helps us heal. It helps us thrive. If you're willing to strap in for this ride, even with the unimaginable pain of child loss, I promise you it's worth it. There will be personal stories, laughs, and shenanigans, but at the heart of this book is one message: allowing yourself to truly be seen by others is the catalyst for deep healing and real happiness—a commodity we're all starving for.

When you finish this book, you'll walk away with a renewed sense of hope and purpose, equipped with tools to improve your life and the lives of those around you.

These are the tools, by name.

- Speak the unspeakable.
- Use your gift to be a gift.
- Don't try to prove yourself, just be yourself.
- The gratitude chain
- Common denominator
- Momentary magic
- The power of being a witness

Our connection is just beginning. Buckle up, buttercup!

PART ONE

THE RISE

W e all have a story of *The Rise*—the time in our lives when everything feels possible—the dream-chasing, the thrill of new beginnings, the moments when the world seems to unfold in our favor. It's a season of joy, discovery, and excitement, when the puzzle pieces of our lives fall into place, even if only for a while.

In this part of the book, I share my own *Rise*. These are the moments that built me, shaped me, and brought me to where I am now. But, *The Rise* isn't just about the good times. It's about the connections we form when life is abundant—the relationships that lift us, the laughter that fuels us, and the dreams that set our hearts on fire. These moments are beautiful, yes, but they're also fragile. And perhaps that's why they're so precious.

The truth is, we all experience a *Rise* in our lives. It may look different for each of us, but it's there—the season of light, of hope, when we feel invincible. Yet, even in these moments, connection is the thread that runs through everything. It's the glue that holds us together in the good times so we have something to cling to when the inevitable storms arrive.

But for now, we celebrate *The Rise*. We honor the joy and hope we feel and the connections we make along the way. Because while this book is ultimately about the healing power of connection, it's important to remember that connection isn't just forged in the fires of hardship. It's also found in the laughter, the love, and the moments when everything feels just right.

This is where my story begins: with dreams, with love, and with the connections that lifted me up in ways I didn't yet understand.

Welcome to *The Rise*.

CHAPTER 1

Broadway Baby

I never wanted to be a mom. You heard me. I'll never forget sitting in the passenger seat of our white '90s station wagon while my mom drove me to Idaho Falls. At the time, we lived in a small town in southeast Idaho called Rexburg. If we ever wanted to go to the mall and do some "real shopping" we had to drive thirty minutes to the nearest booming metropolis of Idaho Falls, or "I.F." as the locals call it.

I don't know exactly why we were driving there. Maybe it was to do some shopping, maybe it was for one of my dance or gymnastics competitions. What I do remember is sitting in the silence, looking over at my mom, and FEELING her sadness. I could tell that life was heavy for her. She had a very difficult childhood, and I don't think that raising four kids in the middle of nowhere Idaho was high up on her bucket list. Being a mother, yes, but doing it in Idaho, not so much. She's a city-lover like me.

The heaviness seemed to cling to my mom like an invisible weight. And even though I was too young to fully understand, I knew something about life had worn her down. This was my first experience with authentic connection, though I didn't realize it at the time: sensing the emotional truth of another person, even in silence.

Looking back now, as a mother myself, I can only imagine the variety of things that could have been weighing on her mind. (And now I'm laughing because I know for a fact that I was an A1 Certified Annoying Shitlin—constantly singing and dancing in the kitchen, fighting with my sister about clothes, talking loudly in weird voices, having a million friends over at the house. No wonder my mom looked like the life had been beaten out of her!) But even then, in that silence, there was connection—this deep, unspoken bond that transcended the chaos and frustration. She might not have been able to express what she was feeling, but I understood her sadness, just like she understood my relentless passion for Broadway.

She used to call me a "raw nerve talking" (I get my superior sense of humor from my mother). NO WONDER SHE LOOKED LIKE THE LIFE WAS BEATEN OUT OF HER. I just remember looking over at her and thinking, "She's too sad. I can tell life is hard and heavy. If that's what motherhood and being in your 40s is like, I don't want it."

It's OK, Mom. I get it now. You were and are a wonderful mother.

Young children never interested me. I didn't have many motherly instincts or desires. All I cared about was being on *the* BROADWAY. It was musicals 24-7 for me. Bice family legend has it that my parents were jolted awake from a deep slumber one night when I was about four years old because they heard someone moving about the house. My dad thought someone had turned on the radio or maybe a burglar had made their way in. There were a variety of loud noises echoing throughout the walls of our home.

They followed the sound and discovered me, short as a four-year-old can be, sitting on the toilet, swinging my feet, singing "The Sun'll Come Out Tomorrow" at full volume. It was 3:00 in the morning. The desire to sing *Annie* in full voice waits for no one.

I believe *Les Miserables* was the first Broadway cassette tape that I owned (just kidding, my sister owned it and I would steal it from her to play on my boom box). Then came *Into the Woods*, *Miss Saigon* (my favorite to this day), *Little Shop of Horrors*, and we can't forget the fabulous and often overlooked off-Broadway hit, *Ruthless* (I'm serious, google it). I believe Brittany Spears was in it. There are some classics from that show.

The amount of time I spent earnestly singing these show tunes in front of the mirror is staggering. Every dance class I took, every voice lesson, every trip to Salt Lake City to see a professional theater production—were all leading me to one end: The Great White Way. Performing was my way of reaching out, of communicating something larger than myself. Authentic connection was my currency—I just didn't realize that the truest form of it wouldn't come through applause but through something much more intimate. The thought of ever becoming a mother one day didn't cross my mind for a second: not in high school, not in college, and only a few times after getting married. I cared about two things: boys and Broadway.

But we all know how this story goes: I became a mom. It happened. Life keeps chugging along and decisions are made. You meet a cute guy in Los Angeles after moving there to teach at a performing arts studio. You fall in love. You get married. You don't make it on Broadway. Whether that's because you only lived in NYC from age nineteen to twenty-one and never moved back, or because of your eating disorder, lack of self-esteem, ADD, total obsession with boys, or lack of belief in yourself, you'll never know.

You may not have found yourself on The Great White Way, but you got yourself a great white guy.

And at that point, that was good enough for me. It was great, in fact.

I was chasing that connection with an audience, with the world, with myself. What I didn't know at the time was that authentic connection isn't something you find only under bright lights or within a standing ovation. It took me decades to understand this, and it wasn't until I met my husband that I realized connection comes in all forms and often from where you least expect it.

I don't think it's a stretch to say that my husband and I are polar opposites. He wanted SEVERAL children, I wanted none. He went to law school, and I majored in musical theater. For decades he was a registered Republican, and I, a Democrat. He loves attending church meetings, I change the lyrics to the church hymns while driving home from the boring meetings and he tells me I'm being inappropriate. He can look at a spreadsheet and his brain still works. I look at a spreadsheet and it feels like aliens have invaded my body and I lose all cognitive function. He tells the kids they need to do what he says, when he says it, no questions asked, and I sit down with the children and dissect their feelings about the situation and rely heavily on sarcasm as a form of discipline. He used to listen to Glen Beck, I barf Glen Beck into the toilet. He's bald. I have great hair. He's methodical and thoughtful. I'm impulsive, impatient, and selfish. I hid in the back of the car to make it look like there were only four of us on a trip to Mexico so we could get a free upgrade to the presidential suite at the resort, but he told the front desk attendant that there were actually five of us and we didn't get the room. How actually dare he have integrity!

But somewhere in that chaos, we found each other. We connected—not despite our differences but because of them. I began to realize that the deepest form of connection doesn't require you to be the same as someone else. It's about seeing the other person fully—messy, complicated, and real—and still choosing to engage, still choosing to share in each other's lives. And I realized, this is the commodity of connection. It's the one thing we have that makes life meaningful, even more than Broadway dreams or fleeting successes. It's why I fell in love with my husband, and eventually, why I became a mom.

I think you're soakin' what I'm spittin' here. So, how did my husband and I end up together?

Picture it: Provo, Utah, 2003. All five feet one inches of me, at twenty-five years old, packed up my 1998 black Honda Accord to drive to Los Angeles, California. I graduated from Brigham Young University with a Bachelor of Fine Arts in Music Dance Theater. I had actually been accepted into my dream graduate program at Boston Conservatory of Music, but then I FREAKED OUT at the thought of graduating with a Master's Degree in Musical Theater and $70,000 of debt. Not to mention, my very fabulous, very gay, somewhat tricky ex-boyfriend had also been accepted into the program, which complicated things (Hi, Rance! Love you!). What on earth was I going to do with that degree when what I really wanted was to be on Broadway? So naturally, moving to LA, land of film and fortune—NOT known for its booming live theater scene—and teaching munchkins how to traipse around stage during *The Wizard of Oz* seemed like a more logical step.

Let's be honest, I had always been taught that getting married and having children was the most important thing I could do with my life. So even though I had the chops to thrive in a graduate program in Boston, finding the right man to complete me and seal my eternal destiny was at the forefront of my mind.

I had lived in NYC as a twenty-year-old and was wholly overwhelmed by the city. This was pre-cell phone, mind you. I had never felt more invigorated, empowered, independent, lost, and lonely at the same time. It left me deflated and drained. I didn't have the confidence, self-awareness, resources, or chutzpah to make another go of it.

So for reasons unknown, I slid my flat white butt into that little black Honda—which had a bright handmade afghan draped over the bulging contents of the backseat—and headed south to find my savior.

I didn't know a soul in the city. I didn't even have a place to live. Luckily, my mother decided to drive with me. And although she was embarrassed to be seen in my borderline beater car, she patiently drove with me from apartment to apartment looking for something that felt safe, welcoming, and affordable. And by the grace of God Almighty and the baby Jesus, we found it.

For 365 days of my life, I lived in a beautiful, clean, cozy apartment right off Santa Monica Boulevard. I made friends. I danced all day. I played on the beach. And I fell in love. I found the man that I thought would complete me and grant me my life's purpose.

CHAPTER 2

Making Moves

As a geriatric (twenty-five! Can you even handle it?), single female living in Provo with a degree in music dance theater (referred to heretowith and henceforth as MDT–that's legal jargon. I know these things because Victor Schmictor is an ATTORNEY), naturally, I was working at Gap and wondering what to do with my life. In the process of girding up my loins to move back to the musical theatre mecca of New York, I received an email from a woman who had seen me perform and was curious to know if I would like to move to Los Angeles for the summer to teach at her performing arts academy. What can I say? It felt right. So very right.

Not only did I end up in a great apartment in a great location in West LA, I had some really great roommates who were privy to the adventurous love story unfolding between Molly Malissa Bice and Victor Michael Jackson—you read his name correctly. And no, he doesn't have rhythm. He's also tone deaf. Just let him have the name.

After getting settled into the apartment as well as a work routine, LA began to feel like home. I spent my days choreographing in the heat, and my evenings at the beach, going on runs in my beautiful neighborhood that bordered Beverly Hills, or attending church activities with other young single adults.

One evening, sweaty and exhausted after a long day of wrangling aspiring young performers, I pulled into our apartment carport. I was greeted by my roommates trying to convince me to go to the Monday night activity at the church. That particular week, it was a car wash. I had two choices: go stinky and sweaty in my dance clothes, or take a quick shower, leaving no time to make myself look beautiful/ presentable to all the eligible bachelors. I opted for the non-smelly but wet version of myself. BOLD, I tell you.

Pulling into the parking lot in my trusty black Honda, I spotted my friend Spencer Hill talking to a Matt Damon looking fellow. Moments after stepping out of my car, Spencer yelled, "Hey Bice! Come over here." I sized up the shortie he was talking to and had the distinct thought, "Small-town wrestler . . . not my type."

But after chatting with him for a few minutes I started to change my tune . . . a little. This Vic character told me he had just graduated from Pepperdine Law School and was studying for the bar exam with his friend Tim every day at the church building so they could take breaks from the grueling process and shoot hoops in the gym. (Most Mormon churches have basketball courts inside their buildings. Is that an odd feature for a church? I surmise that it is and hadn't thought of this before now.) He was kind, genuine, and had a great smile. I recall he was wearing an In-n-Out t-shirt and horrible khaki denim shorts that were faded or stained along the bottom. I also remember thinking it was nice to meet a good-looking guy who didn't seem too focused on his image (thank goodness he married me so my critical self-obsession with how I look and dress could balance us out).

I flitted around to different groups that evening and when we went our separate ways, Vic told me he made the decision to "put me on his list."

He was taking a dating hiatus while studying for the bar so he could improve focus, but he kept a running list of potential ladies to take-a-courtin after the three-day exam—something for this small-town wrestler boy to look forward to. And, well, Little Miss Blue Eyes got herself a spot on his list. If I remember right, there were around seven girls' names jotted down and waiting in the wings. I suppose I was number eight.

However, due to my excellent flirting skills, not only did I get moved to the top of the list, I didn't even have to wait until the bar exam was over.

CHAPTER 3

The Bice Grip

Three weeks later, I came down with strep throat, thanks to the munchkin children I was teaching in *The Wizard of Oz*. Gross kids, am I right? Southern California was just creeping out of June gloom, and after three days in bed, I was spiraling into depression. I was still getting to know people and didn't have many close friends.

On the third day of fever and misery, I called the one person I had instantly bonded with in my church circle, Tracey Thompson. She was a fellow MDT graduate and cut from the same crazy cloth as me. I told her I needed to get out of the house before I lost my mind.

Calling upon my BYU, homemaker-in-training genius, I decided we should make chocolate chip cookies and deliver them to some boys on *my* list (two can play at this game, Victor). To be clear, I didn't have an actual hard-copy list; we're dealing with a perpetually boy-crazy girl here.

Our first stop was to see Bret Ball, a medical student. He seemed . . . nervous. Dare I say, uninterested? I googled him recently. It turns out, he's now a neurosurgeon in Portland, and his wife is an anesthesiologist. I guess he wasn't interested in someone who can still do the splits and moonwalk like a champ in the kitchen. His loss.

Tracey reminded me that Vic and Tim studied at the church building every day. By then, it had been several weeks since our parking lot encounter, and my roommate Jessica Bean kept singing Vic's praises, and I quote, "He's the only true gentleman left in the ward." Mormon congregations are called "wards." So no, I was not in a mental ward—yet.

Around 10 p.m., we pulled into the church parking lot to deliver the baked goods to the two unsuspecting gentlemen studying inside, and my heart began beating out of my chest. Having only met Vic one other time and having only a vague memory of what he looked like, this thunderous thumping surprised me.

Cookies in hand, we made our way to the back door. Sadly, it was locked. Tracey, being less nervous yet equally as unabashed as I, proceeded to wind and whack her way through the bushes and knock on the window of the room where Vic and his law lover, Tim, were studying.

After scaring the crap out of them, Tim made his way down the long hallway to open the door and let us in.

We said our hellos, handed them the cookies, and sat across from them at a large dark oak table. I was directly across from Vic and clearly remember saying to myself, *Wait. He's way cuter than I remember. I think I like him. That's it. I just decided: I like him. I want to go out with him.* This time, he was wearing a Green Lantern t-shirt, not that I knew what that was or what it meant at the time. What I soon learned is that it means he is a good-looking nerd. Our children are now into the Marvel Universe or DC comics, or whatever. It also means that the number one advice I give to anyone who is single is simply, "Find yourself a good-looking nerd. They make the best husbands."

As luck would have it, they were just finishing their studying for the day. It was 10:30 p.m. by this point and, together, the four of us walked out of the building and into the parking lot (the same one where I had declared that Vic was not my type).

Just then, another cute blond girl named Heather pulled up to the church building. What was she doing there, you may ask. Say it with me now: Delivering cookies!! I SHIT YOU NOT. Vic wanted to make sure I included this detail to make it seem he had a slew of girls after him. (Wait a minute—was Heather on the list too?!)

I don't remember exactly what happened, but there was for sure some awkward energy exchanged as she and Vic talked while I stood on the sidewalk with a nervous smile and a large serving of side-eye. She eventually left and I had the spotlight to myself again. Praise the Lord (henceforth and furtherto therefore referred to as PTL).

Tim said goodnight and goodbye at some point, leaving three of us to giggle, converse, and do some cookie nibbling. Being the aforementioned gentleman that he was/is, Vic invited both Tracey and me to go for a ride in his red, vintage, CJ-5 Jeep.

You best believe me when I tell you that while Vic was turned away and tinkering with something in his Jeep, I mimed the "I will slit your throat, you aren't coming with us" motion to Tracey. Gahahahaha. (Please picture me sitting in the corner of the Park City Library right now as I write this, giggling to myself about it and marveling at the caliber of friend I am. Don't worry, she's a fellow MDTer. She understood.)

Ever the actress, Tracey politely declined. PTL we drove to the church in HER car, so she could easily drive home with no fanfare. I climbed into the Jeep to drive off into the July night with my new crush.

The drive started as a simple cruise around the neighborhood, but turned into an escapade on the Pacific Coast Highway (or PCH).

As the Jeep rumbled down the freeway (no doors or windows on this puppy!), the wind blowing through our hair (yes, Vic had hair at the time), we chatted loudly about our families and got to know each other a bit. Vic told me he's the oldest of seven (gasp!), grew up in a small town in Northern California called Calusa, and moved to Mesa, Arizona as a teen. I could tell he was close with his family and had a lot of love for them. That made me feel a lot of love for him.

You can't drive from West LA to Santa Monica, down the scenic PCH, and NOT get out to feel the sand in between your toes. We parked and walked down to the water, chatting all the while. Palm trees, the Santa Monica Pier—with its lit up ferris wheel—and distant mountains were the backdrop to this scene. How could this be real? A cute boy who just graduated law school? Who speaks fluent Spanish? Spending time with me in this beautiful place? Am I dreaming?

That summer of 2003 there was a rare warm current in the Pacific Ocean. To this day, Vic and I argue over the details of what came next. While wading in the water, VIC—Victor, Victor Michael Jackson, VMJ, Victor Schmictor, Victor Victoria, Vicky Poo—IS THE ONE who suggested we jump into the ocean. Do NOT let him try to convince you it was my idea. This is the sandbar I will die on.

"Go for it!" I exclaimed (see? I responded to HIS idea). He pulled off his shirt, kicked off his flip-flops, rolled up his jeans, and jumped in.

Never one to be left out of a good time, I proceeded to shimmy off my Mormon underwear from under my shirt (don't get me started on garments), remove my shirt, and race toward the water in my bra and shorts.

Had I ever worn a bikini top in my life? No. Have I always been critical of my soft stomach and thick arms? Yes. Did I feel comfortable enough on our first night ever hanging out to swim half naked in the ocean with VMJ soon-to-be Esquire? Obvi. And it was oh-so surprising to me!

Splashing and swimming together, the mountains darkly silhouetted by the glow of the full moon, the Santa Monica carousel spinning in the distance, Vic made his way closer to me, wrapped his legs around me and pulled me under the water. *Is he flirting? He's definitely flirting.*

It was magical. It truly was.

I felt like I was in a movie. Honestly, I should have been in some Hollywood movies—is it too late? Did I audition for anything when I lived there? No. (I wish I'd had social media back then to teach me the ways and connect me to the industry better.) I could practically hear the film soundtrack swelling to a crescendo in the background as we laughed at our youthful absurdity. A few spectators gathered to witness the crazies swimming in the dark. It was pure joy and wonderment!

After a solid ten to fifteen minutes, we emerged from the warm salt water, gathered our clothes, and made our way back to his parked Jeep where he had some towels waiting. Going to law school at Pepperdine while living in Malibu will prompt you to carry swimsuits, wetsuits, towels, and surfboards in your car at all times . . . just in case of an "emergency" fun break.

Gentle reader, please picture Vic earnestly, desperately trying to keep his beautiful blue eyes looking STRAIGHT AHEAD and not sneak a peek at my knockers. Yes, they were still safe inside my full coverage black bra, but that doesn't mean they weren't partially exposed. Bless his Mormon, returned missionary heart. He was being so GOOD.

Wrapping a dry towel around my waist, I shimmied out of my soaking shorts, put my dry shirt over my wet bra, and hopped back into his Jeep, taking great care to keep the towel firmly gripped at my side. Ain't no Mormon girl got time to be bottom-half naked on a first (impromptu) date!

Elated and shocked in the best possible way, we drove back to the "west side" where we both lived, just off the 405 freeway and Santa Monica Boulevard. My hair was soaking wet, and Vic thoughtfully loaned me his hat to keep it from whipping me in the face as we drove.

I exited his Jeep with the old side-saddle move and he walked me to the door of my apartment building on Manning Avenue. Standing on my tippy toes, I gave him a one-armed hug, amazed that I had nothing on underneath and had just gone from being on my strep throat deathbed that morning to an ocean baptism of love that night.

This night marked our first true connection, and from that moment on, adventure became a thread that would continue to weave us together. That spontaneous ocean plunge—wet clothes and all—was a metaphor for our relationship: dive in, trust the moment, and let life unfold in ways more beautiful than we could plan.

I was flying. Cloud Nine had arrived.

CHAPTER 4

On My Knees

No, the chapter title isn't what you're thinking, you garbage can. Practically floating, I entered my small apartment and let out a stifled scream. Tiptoeing into Jessica's room, I eagerly woke her up and animatedly stated in a stage whisper, "I'M GOING TO MARRY VIC JACKSON!"

"You were right! He's amazing. So cute! A gentleman. He's smart! We went swimming in the ocean. Oh my gosh! I want to marry him!"

She mumbled an "I told you so" and turned over to sleep. Bless you, Jessica Bean. Bless you.

I have no recollection if I showered before crawling into bed, though I must have—I was freezing and covered in sand—but what I DO remember is lying in bed and realizing I should say a prayer.

But I'm way too tired. Ugh. I just want to go to sleep.

And that's when my BYU, must-find-an-eternal-companion genius kicked into gear again.

I barrel rolled out of bed and knelt on the floor.

"Here's the deal, Big Guy. I will pray on my KNEES every night if you give me Vic Jackson."

I was once a Mormon missionary, serving the people in the Peoria, Illinois Mission. No, I never actually lived in Peoria. That was mission headquarters. I lived in Decatur, Pekin, Effingham—you heard me, Effingham (when my brother heard that's where I'd be transferred to, his response was "Effingham? That's all Mom and Dad gave me for Christmas last year.")—and my favorite city, Kirksville, Missouri. But again, I digress.

The point is that my mission president, Faye Thacker (yes, HIS name was Faye, and his wife's name was Chadley. I couldn't love this fact more), had us read a book called *Drawing on the Powers of Heaven*. The only takeaway I remember was something along the lines that we could "make a deal with God." If you promise him you'll do something, he has to bless you because he is bound by heaven to do so (that's the very watered down version).

And this is exactly what I was doing when I knelt down and asked Heavenly Father to "give me Vic Jackson." I'm not sure I would use that same phrasing today, but it's the best I could do in my exhausted state.

So, for the next ten months, no matter how exhausted I was, no matter how cold the room or hard the floor, I knelt down and PRAYED like you've never heard a good little Mormon girl pray before. Vic's the one I wanted to spend the rest of my life with.

CHAPTER 5

Silling the Dill

The Utah accent is a marvel. For better or worse, much of the world is familiar with it these days because of social media and the booming popularity of Utah influencers (please, don't get me started).

Instead of "deal," it's pronounced "dill." Instead of "real," it's "rill." This is the chapter of how we "silled the dill." Get into it.

Stoked out of my cranium after that moonlit ocean plunge, I waited with baited breath for our next date. We exchanged a few casual calls and texts in the weeks that followed, but no real plans were on the calendar. I knew he was in the final stretch of studying to take the California Bar Exam, and I tried my best to not disturb him.

Jessica and I decided to have a casual movie night at our apartment and I nervously reached out to beach boy with an invite. As luck would have it, the girl he had asked on a date that night had just canceled on him. HE HAD ASKED JENNIFER WHAT'S-HER-NAME ON A DATE TO RECREATE OUR STARLIT SWIM IN THE OCEAN! Can we even believe this, readers?! Our date had gone so well he wanted to repeat it . . . with a different girl! ARE YOU AS

SHOOK, SHOCKED, AND SHAKEN AS I WAS/AM ABOUT THIS? The absolute AUDACITY!

No, I didn't find out this information until a few months later, but I will never let him live this down! Thank you, Jen Volz, for turning him down. I can't even. Did I date multiple guys at the same time? Did I maybe kiss upwards of twenty boys—on the lips—on New Year's Eve? Of course I did. But that literally doesn't even matter or count.

Serendipity was the movie we picked, and the couch is where we sat with blankets and pillows. (Did we have popcorn? Who knows. Who cares.) There may have been a few friends coming in and out, but I only remember it being me, Vic, and Jessica. Bless her heart, having to sit there while two love birds cuddled on the couch. Actually, maybe it was Tracey who watched the movie with us and fell asleep on the floor. It doesn't matter. (Girls, shoot me a text when you read this and let me know.)

At the conclusion of the film, Jessica (or Tracey?) excused herself to go to bed. Holding hands and cuddling alone on the couch, do we think Molly the Unabashed was the one to make the first move? You fool, of course she was!

The specifics are unclear, but I do remember him whispering, "I don't know if we should kiss. I'm not sure it's a good idea. I might not be ready, and I also might not be able to stop if we start." HAHAHAHA, get those lips over here, you idiot.

Gentle listener, a true gentleman he was. He kissed me so tenderly and respectfully, if that is a thing. No tongue. Lots of sweetness. Oh, it was heaven. *Corrupt him, I shall*, I thought to myself. (Nah, it was more along the lines of, *I'll loosen this guy up a bit*. I've been working on that for twenty years.)

The following months consisted of dinner parties with friends, casual dates, long walks, rollerblading on the boardwalk, and lots of making out. His best friend got married that summer, and I caught the bouquet at the reception. Too poetic. He spent long hours playing Settlers of Catan with his friends and I'd pout in the corner. *Oh, Molly, you wee little thing, what an immature thing to do.* I just didn't (and still don't!) like that game. Too slow. Too much strategy. I need fast-paced, action, word-based, clever games. We may have had our first argument about this blasted game. He may or may not have said, and I quote, "I just don't know if I can be married to someone who doesn't like Settlers of Catan." WELP.

Vic still had his "list" and I had a few guys in the back of my mind whom I wanted to take for a test drive to get out of my system to make sure Vic was, indeed, THE ONE. So while things were progressing toward an exclusive relationship, I think we were both a little scared.

After flying to Utah to meet his family, and then a visit to Idaho to visit mine, I freaked out for a hot minute and put things on hold. But deep down, we both knew we belonged together. Dear sweet Jessica helped him pick out a ring (of course, I had expressly told him the *exact* design I wanted) and eight months after our first frolic in the ocean, he proposed to me on that same beach, under a full moon.

"SHUT UP!" were my first words to him after he asked me to be his wife. This is what I wanted, right? *Am I too excited and speechless to process this moment? What is happening?!*

After telling him to shut up a few more times and physically pushing the ring away, he sheepishly looked at me with those dark blue eyes and inquired, "So . . . is that a yes?"

A few more screams and squeals escaped before I pulled myself together enough to confirm, "Yes, I think it's a yes. How is this happening?! YES!" Oh, Victor. The things he has put up with over the years.

Little did we know what we were about to be up against.

On May 29, 2004, ten months after the "baked goods for boys" event, we silled the dill. I was nervous as hell. He wrote the most thoughtful and tender poem and recited it at our wedding luncheon.

First sight, first glance
Thought I'd take the chance

First night, first drive,
You made me feel alive

First swim, same night
Laughter you ignite

First dinner, first date
First call, first kiss
Being with you is bliss

First walk, first talk
First run around the block

First trip, first sing
The CD you decided to bring

First reception, you caught the bouquet
. . . .OK

First gift, first game
Vicky Poo is a cheesy name

First question, first fight
"Settlers," right?

First answers, first vacation
Utah, Albuquerque, the destination

First aquarium, first zoo
I love being with you

First lift, next gift
First rollerblade, first hike
We still have yet to bike

First clean, first cook
First movie, first book
First struggle . . . our jobs
. . . what next

The bar results we celebrate
Thai in the tree
The book—a surprise for me
Thanksgiving, Mexico
Our friends and the lost keys

First Christmas, so sweet
Days I'd gladly repeat

January, still thinking
The break, my heart sinking

Your birthday—a bash
Pink, and in a flash
The flowers, the day—

You stole my heart away.

The song goes on,
To Idaho you were gone
My prayers, my cares,
The decision, the ring.

Back to the spot
Is what I thought

First sight, first glance
This night. Our dance
Thank you for loving me

Today? Begins Eternity

I sang "Unexpected Song" to him, with my friend Alena at the piano. He wore his dad's vintage, chocolate brown three-piece suit. I wore a pink Dillard's special that my mom picked out. A strange salad with avocado and citrus fruit was served. Then we walked over to the Mormon temple, did some weird handshake things while kneeling across the altar, and my destiny was sealed.

Turns out, marriage is hard. It also turns out that thinking that another person can make you whole is also hard—because it isn't true.

OH! And I almost forgot! You better believe that on the night he proposed to me, after I arrived back at my apartment, I flopped on my bed and said a prayer of thanks while LYING ON MY BACK LOOKING AT THE CEILING. My kneeling days were over.

Our first year of marriage was not easy. Oh, let me list the ways:

- law school debt up to our eyeballs;

- merging of two different backgrounds and family cultures (duh);

- the Great Recession;

- Molly's parents separating (they are back together and doing well);

- leaving all of our single friends behind in LA, moving to Salt Lake, and having no new group of friends in Utah;

- an exhausting job working with young kids all day at a summer camp in an old, unairconditioned building in South Salt Lake—I legitimately saw a forty-pound sewer rat wandering the premises on a regular basis;

- old cars in need of regular repairs;

- childhood wounds and trauma to work through with each other;

- fights about paying tithing to our church;

- lingering issues from my decade with an eating disorder; and

- unrealized Broadway dreams just to name a few.

Welp, now that the stage has been perfectly set to welcome our unplanned firstborn child, let us begin.

CHAPTER 6

Pooping Ducks

After moving from LA to Salt Lake City, I got a job as the teen director in the Sugarhouse Boys and Girls Club. After a long, hot summer, I was transferred from the Sugarhouse Boys and Girls Club and asked to help open a new location in Park City. It was perfect. I had been cast in back-to-back shows at the Egyptian Theatre, Vic finally found contract work with a law firm on historic Main Street in Park City, and the way was miraculously paved for us to move to the beautiful resort town that was just coming up for air post-Olympics.

And get this—REAL ESTATE WAS SO AFFORDABLE. It makes my heart weep with regret to think of how many missed financial opportunities and investments we overlooked. We were young. I was dumb. I was scared. I knew nothing about the real world. I could kick ball change until the cows came home, but a mortgage? Renters? Multiple properties on top of law school payments and my non-profit salary? Fuhgeddaboudit. My sweet husband tried to talk me into a few things, and I just played it safe. I just wanted some cute clothes and a stage on which to sing.

Thanks to the factors surrounding the Great Recession, we were able to purchase a darling condominium in the Pinebrook neighborhood of Park City, on stated income. Gentle reader, please know this—the title of "attorney" was looked upon with great promise by our financial lender. And I'd like to take this time to say, bless them. For although this proved to be true (thank you, honey), it took us years before we felt any form of financial stability.

I continued performing at the Egyptian Theatre and running the Park City Boys and Girls Club. One night, while reaching into the spice cupboard to get my birth control pills (just go with it—that's where I kept them), I had the distinct thought: *What would happen if I stopped taking these?*

Please tell me you are laughing right now.

Why this would be considered a "distinct thought" rather than an "obviously stupid question" I cannot say. That's just how it felt at the time. It was more of a, "What if I left this up to fate by not taking my birth control pills? What would happen? Am I even capable of getting pregnant? Is it 'time' to get pregnant? Let's just do an experiment and see!"

This is the part where the "improvising performer whose main goal is to have fun" collides with the "tempting fate with the most serious responsibility on earth" in a pretty serious way. I honestly amaze myself sometimes.

One year and two months after becoming Republican and Democrat—I mean, husband and wife—Vic impregnated me with his Sperm of Great Worth and his natural odor then repulsed me more than conservative talk radio. Is anyone else completely repulsed by their partner's pheromones and body microbiome after becoming pregnant? I made him purchase unscented soap, shampoo, and deodorant. And absolutely no cologne or lotion unless he was longing for an early death. Your body truly knows who created the intense suffering in your womb, and it rebels and repels.

I remember finishing my workday at the Boys and Girls Club in City Park, then making my way up to Main Street on foot to grab dinner before having to perform in *Seussical the Musical!* Between working with snot-nosed kids all day and hoofing it up Main Street at about 8,000 feet of elevation, I was exhausted and STARVING. And what did I want? Mozzarella sticks. And when did I want them? NOW.

This was pre-Siri, pre-Alexa, pre-smartphone days. So while I did have a cellphone, I wasn't able to call every eating establishment on Main Street to find out where I could acquire the needed goods.

Vic was doing contract work at a law firm above a candy store on Main Street, so I popped into his office, grabbed a phone book, and plopped my buttocks upon the floor to start making phone calls.

"Hi. Yes. So, I'm pregnant and I NEED mozzarella sticks ASAP. Is that something you have on your menu?"

"Hi. So, I'm performing in a show in an hour or two at the Egyptian Theatre, but I'm PREGNANT and I will die if I don't get mozzarella sticks. Are you the restaurant that's going to save me? No? OK. Consider yourself a murderer. Goodbye."

At long last, the No Name Saloon came through for me. I'm not sure if your bible mentions the No Name Saloon as the Savior of the World, but mine does. I sat outside on the sidewalk and gobbled those chewy, cheesy, greasy sticks of goodness like my life depended on it. In reality, my husband's life depended on it, as did all of my castmastes' lives. No mozzarella sticks? No life for anyone in my path.

My little Lucy bug grew in my belly while I danced night after night in too tight nude-colored fishnets that had been previously worn by the cast of *La Cage aux Folles*. That's right, I, a pregnant twenty-something, was wearing hand-me-down drag queen tights (I don't want to track down the costume designer to confirm whether or not they had actually been washed). By the time the show closed, Lucy was kicking so enthusiastically in my belly that if I lay on my side while trying to rest, her kicks would shake the entire bed.

I took my final bows, and a few short months later she would make her grand entrance into the world.

It happened on June 11, 2006. She had so much hair on her head that Vic said it looked like I was giving birth to a kitten. According to my mom, Nancy Lee Simmons Hirschorn Bice, I was also born with a gigantic head of dark hair and was nicknamed "Wiglet." Vic, on the other hand, is bald. So . . . I guess you've figured out my secret—I had sex with a cat.

As most newborns do, she looked like an old man for the first few weeks of her life, and Vic lovingly referred to her as Bilbo Baggins. She was blonde, blue-eyed, and entirely helpless.

Meanwhile, I was falling apart at the seams. I didn't bond with her for months. I was a fragile shell of a human being, catapulted into what I later found out is called "self-induced insomnia."

I remember my mom offering to take a few days off from her job as a mental health therapist to help out with the transition to parenthood and Vic and me responding, "Nah. It's OK. We got this. We just want to be together, our little family."

HA

HA

HA

Amazing. I was twenty-eight years old and Vic was thirty-four. How did we have NO CLUE how much time and energy it would take to care for a newborn? Once again, I continued to amaze myself.

I spiraled into intense postpartum depression. My weight dropped to 108 pounds. I was lucky if I got four hours of sleep. I legitimately developed tennis elbow from constantly carrying Lucy's car seat in the crook of my arm and holding her while breastfeeding. Anxiety had a tight grip on me, and I felt as lost as a black gay man on BYU campus.

Vic left his contract job on Main Street and took a job as in-house counsel with a stone company. A stone company? What does that even mean? It was a company that mined rocks from various places and sold them to various people and businesses for landscaping and building. Huh. Who knew? All I knew was that it was new and stressful and strange. They had live ducks walking around, pooping and eating in the front lobby. It was dirty. Industrial. And they gave Vic THREE WHOLE DAYS OFF OF WORK when Lucy was born. America, America, God shed His grace on thee. And crown thy good, with paid maternity and paternity leave, from sea to shining sea.

We lived in a ground-level condo, and one day a pot gut (a sort of small rodent) fell into our window well, chewed through our window screen, and made its way into our pantry. Bleary-eyed, leaking milk or some sort of fluid from every hole in my body, I alerted my knight in shining Mormon-underwear armor that there was an intruder in the house.

Dear reader, this is where Vic's collection of historic SWORDS really came in handy (and yes, he does, indeed, have a sword collection. Please help). He grabbed his samurai sword—the kind disguised to look like a regular walking stick for some historical

Japanese reason—and chased that vermin down the hallway. No success was had. I curled into a ball at the head of our bed, gripping Lucy in my arms, and shrieked at Vic that "girls like boys who have skills!" That's a *Napoleon Dynamite* reference for those of you out of my immediate circle of comedic references.

All of this is to say—those were very strange and exhausting days. I was literally up to my eyeballs in snow, Vic was working a strange and stressful job with stone masons and pooping lobby ducks, I was sleep deprived as hell, and we had no money to speak of.

I'm happy to say that we made it to Lucy's first birthday, thanks to the love and support of family and friends. To make ends meet, Vic had sold his precious CJ-5 Jeep, I had sold my old Honda Accord, and we had purchased one car to share. It was a used Audi of some kind. It was such a great car! It had leather, heated seats and four-wheel drive (which is a must when you live in the mountains), and was very expensive to repair. Eight months after purchasing it, and one day after spending $1,200 to repair it, Vic totaled it while driving down Parley's Canyon (Interstate 80) on his way to work. Did I mention these were stressful times?

But there we were at Lucy's birthday party in our condo's open space pergola picnic table area. It was mostly a celebration for US, not for her. WE had made it. We survived one year as new parents. WHY DID NO ONE TELL ME HOW HARD MOTHERHOOD IS? It isn't talked about enough. Vic's sisters and even our sisters-in-law seemed to take it in stride. They slept when the baby slept. They were out and about four days after the baby was born. Me? Absolutely crushed in every way for a solid year.

Enough about the struggle. Let's get to the good part. After coming up for air after "the year of the baby," good things started to happen. Lucy started sleeping through the night. I started sleeping through the night (thanks to Ambien). Vic changed jobs from the stone company and took a job at a firm in Salt Lake. The pay wasn't great, but it was steady and there weren't any pooping ducks.

Lucy was walking and babbling, dancing and smiling, and was beginning to convince me that this whole motherhood gig might work out after all.

PART TWO

THE FALL

In the grand story of our lives, there are the moments we dream of, and then there are the moments that find us, and they are unwelcome, unplanned, and utterly devastating. I had always thought connection was something to celebrate, something that brought light and joy. Falling in love with Vic, building a family, chasing dreams together—it all felt like the fulfillment of a deep longing to connect, to be seen, and to create a life that reflected that.

But I didn't realize that the truest and most authentic connections are forged not only in celebration but also in sorrow. I never could have imagined that connection would be what saves us when the unthinkable happens.

When we lost Lucy, our world shattered. Everything we had built, everything that seemed steady and sure, crumbled in an instant. But even in that darkness, we found connection—not the kind we had known before, but one that would prove to be more vital than anything we had ever experienced.

Connection became a lifeline. It was the hand that reached out when words failed. It was the silence we shared when grief was too heavy to speak. It was the strength we borrowed from others when we had none left of our own. It was this—this fragile, messy, human connection—that saved us when Lucy lost her life.

And so, while *The Rise* was a story of building love and dreams, what comes next is a story of what happens when everything falls apart. It's a story of survival, heartbreak, and learning that connection is our most valuable commodity—especially when it feels like we have nothing left to give.

It's the story of *The Fall*.

CHAPTER 7

Peter Pan, You Will Grow Up

That fall, I auditioned for the role of Peter Pan at the historic Egyptian Theatre (back then, the Egyptian was a professional equity house, one of only a handful in the state of Utah), and I have to say . . . I nailed it. I even got a pixie cut, flattened my shriveled tea bag boobs down with one of those stretchy flesh-colored medical wraps, and memorized my sides for the callback. And I got the part.

I distinctly remember PLEADING with God to help me get the part. I needed it. I needed an engaging project with creative humans outside of my basement condo. I needed movement and music and expression. Something about this role felt NECESSARY and essential to my soul and my life story. I can't explain it. It was like a magnet pulling me forcefully in. I wanted it so badly. And I got it.

Finally, a role made for a 5'1" amateur gymnast who can sing *and* dance.

Side note to anyone going into theater: if you're a strong singer AND dancer, you will almost always be cast in the ensemble. If you are a great singer and actor but you *can't* dance, you will be cast as a lead. Quit those dancing lessons, ladies. Focus on your acting.

This role was made for me. I'm a solid triple threat. I'm not a standout triple threat or an incredible triple threat, just solid.

I flew across that tiny stage like it was my destiny. And it was— tiny, as well as my destiny. All those years of bulimia, body shaming, not getting the cute boys, not getting the leading roles, having the acne and the big Jewish nose—it was like a fat reconciliation of my soul.

Speaking of flying, we have to take a moment to discuss the actual set up. It starts with a tight harness—think rock climbing harness. I had to step into it like a pair of pants. Although it was custom made for me, that little Venus crotch trap pinched like the dickens. A bit of creative thinking led me to line it with maxi pads in order to soften the pressure of the straps on my pelvis. On the back of my harness was a solid looped piece of metal. That's where the tech crew would attach a sixteenth-of-an-inch wire, strong enough to hold more than ten times my weight. The wire was connected to an intricate pulley system backstage and my flying was initiated by the pull of a rope. And the person in charge of that rope? His name was Daniel Simons.

How exactly Daniel flew me in and out of the shuttered nursery windows, over Captain Hook's ship, across the stage, and to Neverland and back, I don't exactly know. Something about how high up on the rope he pulled? How quickly he released the tension? The amount of tension? I guess we'll never know.

All I know is that I trusted him and that I was having the time of my life. So was my daughter.

Lucy fell in love with all things *Peter Pan*. She'd come to the show dressed as Tinker Bell and be RIVETED the entire time. When the Lost Boys "fell asleep" on stage, she'd tilt her head, close her eyes, and make snoring noises. When Mommy crowed on stage, Lucy put her hands in her armpits, elbows out wide, and flapped her "wings," crowing right along.

Her favorite character was Captain Hook. She would squeal in utter delight every time he came on stage. She called him "Kee Kee" and couldn't. get. enough. Bless my concerned, conservative husband's heart, he genuinely thought she'd grow up to only like the bad boys. She never napped during the show and never disrupted the show. She was LIVING IT. According to my mother, watching Lucy watch the show was better than actually watching the show.

On closing night, one of my castmates gifted me a vintage Peter Pan doll and Lucy flew that puppy all around our condo in what we didn't realize were the final months of her life. "Mommy fly, Mommy fly," she would say, holding it high in her chubby toddler hand, racing around our small living room. We listened to the Broadway cast recording in the car on repeat. We checked out every Peter Pan book from the library we could get our hands on. She'd insist I sing the Captain Hook song over and over again. "Who's the creepiest creep in the world? Captain Hook! Captain Hook!"

I was busy planning Lucy's second birthday party that would be just a few months after the show closed. Yes, of course it was Peter Pan themed. I had even made arrangements for Mark Gallagher, my handsome-as-hell Captain Hook, to make an appearance at the party.

Park City was slowly creeping its way out of another long and intense winter, and on this particular Sabbath day, the 18th of May, it was actually warm enough to not have to wear tights to church—just bare Bice legs . . . exactly the way I like them (of the many bodily features I've picked apart and hated, my legs have never been one).

I remember being so proud that I had taken time to prepare a snack. I'd filled a ziplock bag with animal crackers and sliced a big, red, beautiful apple, which I placed in a tupperware container. The memory of picking out that apple in the produce section of Smith's ended up haunting me for years to come.

Weeks earlier, while foraging for a knife in our kitchen, my mom commented on how extremely subpar our knife collection was. As is often the case with Nancy Bice, she was correct. Days later, she gifted me a fabulous bright blue paring knife. This is what I used to lovingly prepare Lucy's snack that morning. I was being such a good mom! Church! Fruit! Makeup on! Lucy dressed in her bright pink tiny crocs and denim dress! Let's head out the door and live our little lives. Just another day in my charming mountain town with my darling little family.

We made it to church and had to sit near the front. It was a packed house that day, as Bishop John Flint was being released and Bishop Ted Barnes being set apart in his place. On the row behind us sat our dear friends the Kents. The Kent family babysat Lucy once a week so I could teach voice lessons. With all her Lucy exuberance and confidence, she'd don her bright orange-and-pink Carter's snow boots and "help" Steve Kent shovel snow on the driveway. On this Sunday, when she saw five-year-old Joey Kent sitting behind us, she proceeded to put on quite the show, complete with kissing him on the lips. Little did I know, those would be the last lips she'd ever kiss.

As the meeting progressed, so did Lucy's antics. We'd been up late the night before at a wedding and whether she was tired or somehow aware that these were her final moments with us, she became disruptively inconsolable. Before long we carted her energetic bundle out to the foyer for distraction and consoling. She was throwing a pretty impressive tantrum, sometimes referred to as "The Great Tantrum of '08."

Here is a short list of things we attempted to snap her out of her meltdown:

- pushing her on the old metal swings in the churchyard,

- offering her cookies,

- singing to her,

- chasing her down the hallway,

- tickling her,

- holding her, and

- walking her around the building.

At one point, I vividly remember her sighing in desperation and laying her head on Vic's strong shoulders, only to pop up again moments later and look at me with tears in her eyes. I have full confidence that when I see her in the next life she will confirm that yes, she was reluctant as hell to let us go. Somehow, she knew this was her assignment and destiny. It was eating her up knowing her spirit wouldn't be with us much longer. It's painful to write this. My eyes are wet as I sit in Persephone Bakery in Jackson Hole typing these words. Vic just glanced over and then put his head in his hands.

After repeated failed attempts to appease her, it was evident she wasn't going to settle down, so we made the decision to leave early. Vic had driven to church separately, so I headed to my trusty silver Honda Civic and got her strapped into her car seat. Once I was in the driver's seat, I twisted around and handed her the container of thinly sliced apples I had prepared. She had mostly stopped crying by this point, and I could only assume that the little peanut was hungry and exhausted. The occasional shuddering, whimpering aftershocks of a strong cry occasionally passed through her lips.

As I began turning the key in the ignition, I heard her choking. It wasn't your average, "something is kind of stuck in my throat" sound. It was primal and different and scary as hell.

Immediately, I turned the car off, jumped out, opened her door, unbuckled her from her car seat, and yelled for Vic, who was across the parking lot. He raced toward us, assuring me everything would be OK, no need to panic. He took Lucy into his strong arms and began administering the Heimlich maneuver. That's when her big blueberry eyes locked with mine. A look of panic and confusion washed over her face. "Come on, honey! It isn't working!! WHAT IS HAPPENING?!" That's when a green Subaru pulled into the parking lot and I screamed "My daughter is choking! We need help!!"

Luckily, the Pinebrook fire station is right next door to the church building. I saw my husband RACE with Lucy in his arms to their front door. When Vic was a child, his younger brother, Sam, choked on a marble. His mom draped Sam over her arm and ran out the door to their car, jarring and bouncing him with every panicked step. Just as she reached the car, the marble popped out. With this memory in the back of his mind, he ran with Lucy folded over his forearm, certain that the result for Lucy would be the same.

Desperate and panting, he arrived at the fire station door. With his one free hand, he grabbed the door handle—access to the help we needed—only to discover it was locked. He ran around the corner to find another door that would surely grant him access. He peered in the windows searching for someone. He ran back to the west door and pounded and pounded and POUNDED on the glass. Someone had to be there, right? It's a fire station! They save people! Somewhere in the pounding and searching, Vic felt Lucy go limp. Fighting the nightmare assaulting his mind he thought, *OK, it's OK. Lucy's not afraid now. We have a chance to fix this. She's still getting some air. It will be OK. We just need a second to fix this.*

At this point, witnessing Vic's panic and Lucy's pale body, blood began flowing away from my extremities as I declined into panic. I could not feel my limbs. They were tingling and numb, while the weight of a thousand broken dreams crushed my chest. Church goers, including medical professionals, doctors, nurses, and the head of Summit County search and rescue, began pouring out of the church building.

I began bargaining out loud with God through a cascade of anguished tears. "I will do anything! I promise I will be more honest and kind. I will pay my tithing!" In the Mormon faith, we are asked to pay 10% of our increase to the church in order to help build the kingdom of God. This has been a long-standing point of contention in our marriage. "I will do whatever you ask, God! Please, please don't take my Lucy. I will give up everything. I will be perfect and obedient. Help! I beg of you! PLEASE, NO!"

Someone called 911 as I lay on the grass, spiraling into an all-consuming darkness and despair that defies description. A voice cried out, "Does anyone have a pocket knife?!" There was discussion of doing an emergency tracheotomy. It didn't happen, but it was discussed. I remember hearing about a specific version of CPR that was being performed next, where pressure points near her groin were rubbed in order to instigate blood flow. (I don't know, I'm an actress, remember! Insert sobbing emoji. I knew next to nothing of these medical terms at the time.)

A group of about three women, including a teenage girl named Sammy, attended to me while I wailed in agony on the fire station lawn. Of course it's all a blur, but I remember them being so gentle and soothing, stroking my arms and legs as I mumbled about how strange my limbs felt. Someone cradled my head and reminded me to breathe. Never had I displayed or experienced such complete helplessness and unfiltered agony in my life.

In that moment, it was as if Daniel, whom I had complete trust in, who had been flying me across the Egyptian Theatre stage, had sliced the rope in one clean swoosh of a dagger and I'd plummeted to the stage floor in a heap of despair. The show absolutely could not go on.

While women tried mightily to comfort me, another group of people formed around Lucy's little body. Vic laid his hands on her head and proceeded to pray over her, offering her a desperate blessing. Neither of us can remember what was said. Vic tells me he only remembers feeling uninspired, muddled, helpless, and confused.

Eventually, the firemen did arrive. We later found out they were grocery shopping! No one had stayed behind to man the station! I suppose the emergency doesn't usually come to them? They are trained to go TO the emergency (we can save this discussion for another day.) The firemen, who are also trained paramedics, proceeded to intubate Lucy. Moments later, a life flight helicopter landed and whisked my daughter away.

In an instant, I was banished from Neverland forever and forced to grow up in a very real and painful way. No amount of pixie dust could get me back.

CHAPTER 8

Faster than a Helicopter

As the edges of reality continued to blur, Vic had the wherewithal to make his way to a car with our dear friend Brad Hale. Brad was one of the doctors on the scene. He was also part of the other family from our church congregation and neighborhood who watched Lucy for me once a week so I could teach voice lessons. Lucy would spend one day a week with the Kents and one day with the Hales. She loved them and their respective children.

Brad and Vic proceeded to race down Parley's Canyon to Primary Children's Hospital (in Salt Lake City). Meanwhile, a couple of men swiftly and lovingly lifted me up, thoughtfully draping one of their suit coats over my legs (bare Bice legs, remember?) and carried me to Susan Hale's black Suburban. Susan is a nurse, Brad a doctor, and both of them are incredibly good, kind, generous people.

Another woman from church named Claudia Redd hopped in the back of Susan's car with me while Susan drove. Claudia is a sweetheart from El Savador with an endearing accent and the most beautiful skin you've ever seen. But you know what isn't beautiful? Her singing voice. In an attempt to comfort me as I lay in her lap, she stroked my hair. At one point she began singing "I Am a Child of

God," a classic Mormon children's primary song. Despite my frantic state, the true Molly in me whimpered, "Please stop. That isn't helping."

With Susan confidently at the wheel, I mumbled in the backseat something about wanting to call my family. My dad's number was the only one that came to mind. I have no memory of what I said when he answered. I think my parents were visiting my sister in Michigan at the time.

Unable to walk when we arrived at the hospital, I was escorted inside in a wheelchair. My firstborn child, my flesh and blood, the tiny human being who made me a mother, was here one moment and then . . . on death's door the next? Because I FED HER FOOD TO KEEP HER ALIVE? My nervous system was shattered.

At this point, I allowed myself to hope for the tiniest sliver of a miracle. *We are at the hospital! I was told she was still "alive." Maybe there's a chance!*

While being wheeled down the hospital hallway (who pushed me? Was it hospital staff? Was it my friend Susan who had driven me down the canyon?), we ran into an ER doctor who I think was on the team of medical professionals who admitted Lucy. He could have been on the lifeflight team, he could have been a med student. All I know is that I viewed him as my possible savior, a miracle worker who would tilt my world back to its former axis.

I slowly stood from the wheelchair and wrapped my arms around him in relief. "Is she going to make it? Where is she? Did you save her? What's going to happen?" Stunned, he looked at me in confusion, with a bit of sadness in his eyes. He replied with something to the effect of, "We don't know yet."

And thus began four days of anguish like I never knew was possible. It turns out, it would be YEARS of anguish, but the days we were in the hospital I could count. As I sit here writing this in the Park City summer sunshine, I'm thinking of the families in Gaza and Israel. It is my firm belief that the body and mind are not meant to endure or adapt to such trauma. It is beyond the pale, beyond the nervous system, beyond the soul's ability to make sense of our mortal existence. The all-encompassing PTSD I still experience from time to time—I'm having an episode as we speak—feels as if it has affected me on a cellular level.

This isn't to say healing isn't possible. But it is to say that loving others and living with a sense of peace and safety is our birthright. When those innate needs are betrayed and manipulated, we often struggle to recognize our very selves.

Forty minutes after arriving at the hospital, when we were finally allowed into Lucy's room in the Pediatric Intensive Care Unit (PICU), I couldn't find the strength to enter. Vic immediately raced to her side. He was able to *not* look away and to face the truth in front of him. He had an inner strength I couldn't seem to find. My fear slipped into the driver's seat and was taking me on an erratic joy ride. The thought of what I would see behind the curtain had me in a chokehold. (Wait, am I allowed to use that term when my daughter choked to death?)

Someone (Brad Hale?), led me from the PICU family waiting area through the wide double doors into the PICU, and around the corner to Lucy's hospital bed. I drew the curtain back and saw a shell of my husband stroking Lucy's hair, holding her hand, tears streaming down his face. "She's beautiful," he uttered from his chair when he heard me enter.

As if wearing a weighted vest in water, I slowly made my way to her bedside. A sweet nurse with mousy blonde hair gave me a heartbroken half smile. She worked quietly, offering us as much dignity, grace, and privacy as she could in the cramped space.

After hearing Vic call me by name a few times, and after hearing us speak of our beloved Lucy to each other, she shyly spoke up and asked, "I'm sorry, is your name Molly?"

"Yes."

"My name is also Molly. And my daughter's name is Lucy."

A beat.

Vic and I looked at each other, confused.

"Well, our Lucy's name is actually Lucia," we said. "But, wow, what a coincidence."

"My daughter's full name is also Lucia" she said, a look of awe washing over her face.

"Your daughter seemed so familiar to me when they brought her off the helicopter. But I had no idea where I knew her from. I still don't know. I don't live in Park City, and I've never met you, but I know your daughter."

Our connection would prove to be even stronger and stranger in the coming days and years.

Someone, or something, was aware of us. We were instantly connected. As a writer and creative expressor, names and words are meaningful to me. It's why we carefully chose our children's names, and it's how the Divine continues to wink at us.

CHAPTER 9

The Yellow Line

The next four days were spent in a barrage of comings and goings. That first day, many of our friends from church visited the hospital, still in their Sunday best after racing down not long after the life flight helicopter took off. Neighbors, college friends, even some of my former colleagues from the Boys and Girls Club also paid us a visit. How did word spread so fast? That's right, I posted something on Facebook about it. Or maybe I asked my beautiful friend Anna Evenson to write a post for me?

I wasn't eating. I wasn't sleeping. I couldn't think straight. It took all of my cognitive function to simply breathe. Because we raced to Salt Lake in a panic, we had no clothes, underwear, contact juice, or clean socks. I have no idea who in our church family took charge. Someone assigned Alexandria Redd, a young teenage girl, to be the person to pack some essentials for us. She grabbed everything I would have: soft sweats, comfortable T-shirts, face wash, and Vic's favorite socks. I don't know if it's because she speaks Spanish or not, but she grabbed a brown Sarah Jessica Parker brand T-shirt (remember when she had a brand for a hot minute? I believe it was called "Bitten") that had a sun on it with the word "LUZ."

Luz means "light" and the word the name "Lucy" is derived from. It's one of the reasons we chose to name her Lucia, the other reason being Queen Lucy the Valiant from *The Chronicles of Narnia*.

Little did I know when I purchased the shirt that I would be wearing it as I held Tinkerbell in my arms for the very last time.

It was on day two that they decided to do surgery and go into her lung to remove the apple piece. My brain told me that once the apple slice was gone, she'd be able to breathe and function properly again! Right?! *There's an obstruction now, but then it will be gone. So she'll be able to breathe again!* My thinking was so rudimentary, so grasping.

They brought the apple piece out in a small jar with a screw-on blue lid. It was so tiny. How can something so small cause such a gigantic traumatic impact? It was the size of my pinky nail! What I didn't realize at the time was how quickly and easily an apple piece made of so much water can disintegrate. Initially, the apple piece she aspirated was larger, but not much. So, while I was hopeful that she could make a miraculous comeback after the sliver of life-giving fruit was removed, what I forgot was that she had been without oxygen for far too long.

In fact, my hope was so strong that I actually had the idea to encase the apple piece in some sort of gold and keep it as a token of the time Lucy "almost died." The mind just cannot comprehend and accept the sudden death of a perfectly healthy child. Any child! It goes against our very nature, and it takes years of peeling back layered anguish before a parent can find even just a moment of peace with this reality.

More testing and scans took place, and it was determined her brain activity was next to nothing. The swelling around her brain was too great. Unless it decreased rapidly, this was the end of our time on earth with our Lucy Sweet, our firstborn flesh and blood.

Family and a few close friends gathered in her room. The nurses pinned a pink butterfly on the curtain outside her door to indicate this was a sacred space, a final goodbye. It told the hospital floor that a fairy was gaining her wings.

Was it one of the nurses who painted her toenails pink? Maybe it was some of Vic's sisters? We gave her a tender sponge bath, covering her in kisses and salty tears all the while. My mom suggested we cut locks of her sunlit strands of curly hair.

The end was here.

It's too much, isn't it? It's too much.

Among those standing strong and stoic in solidarity and support was our dear friend Justin. Not only was he there to hold us while we cried but he brought fresh food from the restaurant he managed, Cucina Toscana (now called Valter's Osteria), for my family to feast on. BECAUSE DID I MENTION THAT ON DAY TWO OF LUCY'S HOSPITAL STAY IT WAS VIC'S BIRTHDAY? Can you even imagine? Oh, my Vic. His shattered heart.

Lying in the hospital bed on either side of our daughter, Vic and I surrounded her with equal parts love and anguish as people around the room shared thoughts and memories of our little Tinkerbell.

I started my remarks the same way I started this book: "I never wanted to be a mom. Or at least, that's what I thought. But I'm grateful I am one. Lucy changed me. She taught me more than I could ever have imagined. I'm proud to be her mom."

I don't remember what else I said. I don't remember what Vic or my parents or in-laws said. But I can picture all of those beautiful faces surrounding us—my siblings, Vic's siblings, Brad and Susan Hale, Steve and Kalisa Kent, and my dearest friend, Justin Kinnaird—all of them standing as sentinels to Lucy's life. I do remember the moment the organ donation team came to take her. My incredible, sensitive, thoughtful husband told me I should be the last to hold her in my arms. He lifted Lucy and placed her in my lap on the bed, my small hands embracing her with her in the same position in which she came into the world.

Honorable and strong, Vic wheeled us down the hallway toward the surgical room. We were told once we reached a large yellow line across the floor we would not be able to go any further. Giving my daughter's body away at that yellow line and slowly peeling myself out of the bed into a precarious standing position was the most difficult thing I've ever done in my life. And I pray to God it is the hardest thing I will ever have to do.

Standing at the yellow line, the boundary between what was and what would never be again, I realized I was crossing into an unimaginable new reality. That line wasn't just a physical barrier; it was a threshold that marked the separation of worlds—the one where Lucy lived and the one where she didn't. I had no choice but to step across, even though every fiber of my being screamed to stay.

Life, I've learned, is full of these lines we don't want to cross, moments that demand we let go of what we love most and move forward into the unknown, even when we feel wholly unprepared. The yellow line will always be etched into my memory as the moment I let go, not of my love for Lucy but of the physical connection I so desperately wanted to hold onto. It was the ultimate act of surrender, and in that surrender, I found the first flickers of grace.

Barefoot and dazed, I padded my way down the cold and barren hallway into the waiting arms of my mother—the mother whom I sat next to in that white station wagon all those years ago thinking about how exhausted and sad she looked. (Who's exhausted and sad NOW, sister?) Steady and sure, she held me while grieving not only the loss of her beautiful granddaughter but my unutterable pain.

Her strength didn't erase my pain, but it reminded me that even in my darkest, most vulnerable moments, I wasn't alone. My mother had always been my first connection, and in this moment of unimaginable loss, she became my lifeline once again.

Because we were unable to be in the room with Lucy, I asked Nurse Molly to stand in as my representative. I didn't want my baby in there alone. She was having major surgery to remove her organs and she needed her mommy there, her Peter Pan.

It's unbelievable to me that there was a fellow Molly mom with a fellow Lucy daughter able to stand as witness for me in the final moments of my daughter's life. While standing in the corner of the room during the procedure, she said it was extremely sacred, heart-wrenching, and painful. My daughter was sacrificing her body to help others live.

Her liver went to a six-month-old baby girl and her kidneys to a thirty-eight-year-old father with four children.

Dear Mr. & Mrs. Jackson,

On behalf of the staff of Primary Children's Medical Center and Intermountain Donor Services, may I extend to you and your family our sympathy in the recent loss of your daughter, Lucy. I appreciate your compassion and generosity in allowing her participation in the donor program during this very difficult time.

Although it cannot compensate for your loss, I hope you will find some comfort in knowing that through the gift of donation you and your family have brought new hope to many individuals awaiting transplants. I would also like to share with you a little about the recipients.

Lucy's kidneys were given to a 38-year-old man from California. He is married and the father of four children. He works in construction. He spent five-and-a-half years on dialysis. He is recovering at home and doing well.

The liver went to a 6-month-old baby girl also from California. She is an only child. She is doing well and enjoying normal baby activities.

All donated tissues undergo medical tests to determine their suitability. The majority are ultimately utilized for transplantation to improve and enhance lives. Assuming Lucy's tissues can be transplanted, her heart valves may be used to help two separate individuals suffering from severe valvular disease.

Words alone cannot express the love and gratitude of the recipients. These precious gifts have not only touched their lives but the lives of their family and friends as well. Thank you.

Sincerely,
Chuck Zollinger RN, BS, CPTC
Organ Procurement Coordinator

Years later, I was speaking to a group of medical professionals at an event at the University of Utah. Nurse Molly was in the audience. I couldn't believe it was her. I hadn't seen or spoken to her since the hospital and had no way of getting in touch due to HIPAA laws.

We embraced in the hallway after my speech. With tears in her eyes she told me:

> I have thought of you so much since that day. Lucy was, and still is, my only organ donation patient. It is very rare for a "regular" nurse to be in the room when they harvest someone's organs. I want you to know I was very scared when you asked me to stand in for you. But I stood in the corner of the room. I stood in your place for you. I tried to be strong. It has had such an impact on me. I have had to remind myself over and over that THIS IS NOT MY PAIN, this was not MY Lucy. I have literally felt your pain as if it were my own. I have thought of you and Vic again and again and again. I was so honored to stand for you when you couldn't.

I then told her we have a son named Peter who joined our family eleven months after Lucy left earth.

That's when she looked at me and said, "You are kidding. That's my husband's name."

> Lucia Isabella Jackson
>
> "Lucy"
>
> Lucia Isabella Jackson, "Lucy," of Park City, passed away at Primary Children's Hospital, Thursday, May 22, 2008, after a tragic accident. Lucy was born June 11, 2006, in Salt Lake City, UT, to Victor Michael and Molly Bice Jackson. Lucy fell in love with Peter Pan and Captain Hook

after watching her mother fly above the stage in the role of Peter. Lucy loves "juiccccce," jumping, dancing, feeding horses, and playing with friends and family. Her little body wasn't big enough for her exuberant and lively spirit which illuminated all who met her. Her name means "light" and she lives up to her name in every way.

Lucy is survived by her parents, Vic and Molly; grandparents, Le and Marlene Jackson and Russell and Nancy Bice, and many aunts, uncles and cousins who love her. We anxiously await her glorious resurrection so we can be together again.

We are so grateful to the wonderful doctors and staff at Primary Children's Hospital who took such good care of our little Lucy during her last few days in mortality. We have felt the love and prayers of family, friends, and caring communities who held and sustained us during these difficult days. Thank you.

Funeral services will be held Tuesday, May 27, 2008, at the Park City LDS Stake Center, 2300 Monitor Drive beginning at 11:00 a.m. A viewing for friends and family will be held Monday, May 26, from 6 to 8 p.m. at the Kimball Ward Building, 2555 W. Kilby Rd., and at the Park City Stake Center from 9:30 to 10:30 a.m. on Tuesday morning. Burial will be at the Salt Lake City cemetery. In lieu of flowers, friends have established a special fund. Donations to the "Lucy Jackson Fund" will be accepted at any Utah branch of Chase Bank.

The world didn't break—it shattered. Like glass dropped from an impossible height, every piece of me fragmented, scattering into the dark unknown. The weight of grief was unbearable, a suffocating gravity that pulled us under, deeper and deeper with each breath, each heartbeat, each silent scream. There was no putting us back together. We were broken beyond repair, beyond hope.

In those first few days, it felt like no amount of light could penetrate the thick, relentless fog that surrounded us. We were drowning, gasping for air. And yet, it was in those very moments— when our lungs ached for breath—that hands reached out, strangers and loved ones alike, gripping us tight. They held us up when we couldn't stand, spoke when our voices failed, fed us when food was unimaginable.

Connection wasn't some far-off ideal, something we pondered over in better times. It was raw, immediate, vital. It was the only thing that kept us breathing, the thin thread we clung to as we teetered on the edge of an abyss. Without it, we would have been lost, swallowed by the emptiness. But with it, piece by shattered piece, we began to survive.

CHAPTER 10

The Juice

Let's get to the juicy stuff . . . marriage. How does a marriage survive the loss of a child? There is a statistic that gets thrown around like candy at a parade claiming that 80% of couples who lose a child separate or divorce. Honestly, this sounds believable, and if you're one of these couples, I understand why. I'm not sure how this percentage became so prevalent, but it's false. According to The Compassionate Friends organization, "the truth is that only 12–16% of marriages end in divorce after the death of a child, believed to be from the "shared experience" of the death (from www.compassionatefriends.org, "To the Newly Bereaved," 2016). In some rare cases, death of a child can even bring couples closer together. Who else on God's green earth is going to share the same specific trauma surrounding a human being of your own flesh and blood? There is no other human alive who loves your deceased child as much as you and your partner.

That being said—hold onto your butts!

Marriage is already hard. Period. If it isn't hard for you, congratulations. You deserve a special place in hell where the devil will pin a rose on your cute little button nose. Good-for-freaking-you.

Guess what else is hard? Being single. Also—being alive. Even a marriage of two like-minded people—who love, respect, and admire each other, who have more than enough money, decent health, good jobs, and great friendships—is fraught with life stress, dental appointments, car issues, differing opinions, indigestion, flight delays, snoring, sickness, and having to decide where to go for dinner.

It would be absolute fiction to think that a child dying wouldn't affect a marriage. So, let's speak the actual truth.

I don't need to tell you about the unrelenting stress, trauma, and grief of losing a child. Imagine mixing that into your marriage. Imagine two adults who are supposed to take turns providing support and strength to each other, but both are rendered entirely nonfunctional at the same time. We were zombies—sleepless, weary, drowning-in-trauma-and-grief zombies. How were we expected to take care of one another?

It was during this time that I had the realization that maybe I was supposed to pursue that New York Broadway dream after all. CLEARLY, this union was not sanctioned by God, or anyone, because anything that was THIS painful was not meant to be. We had given it the old college try (what does that phrase even mean?), and it didn't work out. This was my one chance to escape and start over! This was a sign that I was living the wrong life . . . the life that was never meant for me.

I entertained this thought for a few hours one day while Vic was suffering at work. I was sure this plan to escape would make me a new person and magically end my suffering. I'd no longer be a shattered thirty-year-old who was unable to sleep at night. I'd be reborn as a Broadway babe, spending my evenings strolling through

Central Park and laughing with friends. I'd even leave my high-demand religion and reinvent myself.

But I knew this was a pipe dream, just a desperate attempt to outrun my pain. I still loved Vic. I chose to stay. I couldn't abandon him in his pain. The ache in my soul would follow me wherever I went.

Looking back, I cannot believe we'd only been married for FOUR YEARS when Lucy died. Four tiny little years. I was thirty years old! Still a baby myself. Our marriage was a toddler. We were still learning to run and ride a bike without training wheels. We didn't even know how to swim or read or write yet.

And here we were, utterly drowning. One stormy spring day, we were driving down the winding canyon road from Park City to Salt Lake, the rain falling in sheets. The skies were angry and thunder shook the car. I think we were driving to pick out and design Lucy's headstone. The car was filled with nothing but silence and heartache. Neither one of us cared how fast we were going, what the visibility was like, or how bald our car tires were.

We looked at each other and almost simultaneously said, "Wouldn't it be great if we just got in a car accident and died?"

We dripped with envy when looking at elderly people. "They've made it! They don't have much longer to go. They will see their loved ones soon. I want to be them. How can we live another day, yet alone another several decades?"

The funny thing about grief is that although you no longer recognize yourself and you feel as if your brain has been invaded by an alien virus, your body mostly carries on as before, as far as basic functions. You still need to eat, although you likely won't have an appetite; you still need to poop; you still need to sleep, something I still struggle with fifteen years later; and sometimes, you still want to have sex.

Vic and I had KIND OF, SORT OF, MAYBE, *MAYBE* thought about trying to have another child before Lucy's accident . . . but I wasn't ready. Now that she was gone—now that I realized that I HAVE NO CONTROL OVER MY OWN LIFE AND GOD IS GOING TO GIVE AND TAKE AND DO WHATEVER THE HELL HE WANTS—why not have unprotected sex and just see what happens. (Wait, isn't this what I did when I got pregnant with Lucy? I'm a planner!)

My thoughts were these: if I am not in charge of my life, then I'm just going to roll the dice and let life do whatever it wants with me. It was a strange mix of peaceful surrender and anger, a giant middle finger to the universe.

Six weeks after we buried our daughter, I was pregnant with our son. On April 8, 2009, I gave birth (UNMEDICATED!) to a broad-shouldered boy (IT HURT!). Outside the rain-splattered hospital window was a rainbow, a message from Neverland. I stared at my son all night. I was still in shock that my firstborn was dead. I still couldn't sleep.

Remember how I had severe postpartum depression after Lucy was born? We are going to make a layered cake here and add a crippled nervous system on top of postpartum depression on top of insomnia on top of a body that just made another body—and then pushed that little body out—on top of grief and heartache. I was a multi-layered, hot mess, double espresso express.

Vic told me one day that he honestly expected to come home from work and find me dead on the floor. I was a SHELL of a human being. Vic was too. But, he was sleeping better than I was and wasn't dealing with pregnancy hormones, breastfeeding, and adjusting to new antidepressants. How Peter survived this, I will never know. While I was pregnant, one woman told me he was absorbing my sadness in utero. Welp, sorry 'bout that. Not much I could do, bruh.

I remember my dear friend Susan Hale commenting how sad she was for me because I was being forced to grow up so fast. This comment caught me off guard because I thought, *What is she talking about? I'm a thirty-year-old woman! I'm pretty grown. . . .* Oh, Molly. You were just beginning your journey of growth and expansion. Susan was right.

We returned to couples therapy a few weeks after the funeral. I sat down on the couch and asked, "Now, remind me, what was such a struggle before our daughter died?"

Whatever our differences and arguments were before our daughter's death, they paled in comparison to the insurmountable feat of simply wanting to continue living life. It seemed laughable that we had previously sought counseling. What we now faced was THE BIG ONE.

We were both on edge. Our brains were changing. We were depleted in every way. We argued often. Vic didn't have the time to grieve deeply because he had to go to work. He envied that I could stay home and cry my eyes out if I wanted to. **This is where one of my brilliant readers needs to be inspired to research and write an entire book on grief culture in America and how employers need policies in place when an employee suffers traumatic loss, along with offering emotional intelligence seminars and a culture of safety and authenticity. Can someone more business-y than me please write this book?**

Not only did we go to couples therapy, we also saw therapists one-on-one. We really were committed to our healing, but that doesn't mean it was easy.

Grief is WORK, especially in individualistic America where we have so few rituals to represent our anguish. Then layer on being a member of a religion that strongly believes in life after death and that "families can be together forever." While this "knowledge" can bring some peace, it also has an undercurrent and implication that members of the church don't feel as much pain as the general population of humans. PSHAW, I say to this, PSHAW!

More than once, Vic cried in his SLEEP. That's how strongly the trauma and grief gripped his body and mind. He dreamed one night we were at Disneyland, and he was so excited to show Lucy some princess snow globes on display in the castle. He went to pick her up to show her the beautiful snow globes that were lit up in various colors, and she wasn't there. His arms were empty. I remember the bed shaking as stilted sobs escaped his body. He couldn't let it out during the day or he wouldn't be able to function at work. It was cruel.

Vic has struggled with depression since his law school days. He battles it on a deeper and more intense level than I do. I am naturally optimistic, upbeat, fun, and energetic. I'm a doer. Vic is a thinker and deep feeler. Lucy's death shattered both of us, but the residual grief and sadness lives deep in Vic's being. He doesn't have as many friends to talk to, as many outlets, and words don't come as quickly to him. He lives in his head a whole freaking lot. Frustrated, I often want to shake it out of him, loosen him up! What I'd give to see Vic drunk or high. He is wound so tightly. He keeps me in line and I force him into the conga line.

Marriage is strange to me. I highly value independence. Yes, I'm an extrovert in many ways, but I need alone time, away from all stimuli, on the regular. Once upon a time, back in the '90s, I took a personality test, and I was classified as a "yellow." According to this particular test, a yellow personality is motivated by FUN. If something isn't fun, it isn't worth doing. Vic, on the other hand, is a "blue"—motivated by intimacy.

I remember being on the phone with my mom in the first few months of our marriage. I was pacing around our little apartment talking about who knows what, just chewing the fat. When I popped back into our bedroom, Vic was sitting silently on the bed looking hurt. I had no idea what he could be upset about. After some prodding, he told me he felt left out that I had walked out of the room to talk with my mom. Why didn't I put it on speaker phone and stay in bed with him? (Insert wide-eyed emoji here.)

He wants to run errands with me, hang out with me in the mornings while he gets ready for work, and hear details about conversations. . . . It's sweet but feels smothering at times. The truth is that much of the time I want to travel with friends, be in another show, do my own thing. If he and I happened to cross paths during our independent busy schedules, GREAT! He wanted our schedules intertwined. I wanted him to have more friends, more hobbies. He wanted me to have fewer. In many ways, we are fundamentally so different.

BUT, BUT, BUT—in the deepest ways, we are so alike. We know grief so intimately and have had such powerfully tender experiences together. We know our firstborn—the tiny being that made us parents—like no one else on earth. And we have experienced the profound truth uttered by LDS apostle Neal A. Maxwell when he said,

"The cavity carved by pain can one day become our receptacle for joy" ("But for a Small Moment," September 1, 1974).

What does this look like for us?

Opening presents on Christmas morning with Peter and Zoë and quietly crying from the overwhelming sense of peace we feel as they scream with excitement. Despite our differing worldviews or beliefs, despite our personality differences and values, we always get hit at the same time with a wall of gratitude for this little family of ours because we never thought we'd experience everyday moments of "normalcy." You want to see me lose my shit? Come to one of Zoë's dance recitals or Peter's orchestra concerts. Our cavity has been carved so deep that the smallest ounce of parental pride and love nearly knocks the wind out of us.

Or on our vacation to Europe, we held hands in the autumn sunshine while walking across the Charles Bridge in Prague. Live music was playing, tourists snapping photos, kids squealing, vendors vending, the leaves in full fall splendor. Silently, we squeezed each other's hands, overcome with emotion at the beauty of life and our remarkable journey.

When we made it to the end of the bridge, we held each other and cried. We didn't need to explain anything to one another. We knew. Lucy was with us. Life was on our side. Love was on our side. The cavity carved by our pain was now overflowing with joy.

I was telling my dear friend Kelley Wolf how Vic and I get hit at the same time, every time, with this crazy cocktail of sadness and gratitude because of the pain we experienced. I told her there are times I almost feel sorry for people who haven't gone to the depths we have because I wonder if they feel joy in the same way we do. Not that joy (or sorrow, for that matter) is a contest—there is no barometer for pain—we just know life the way it exists for us.

I'm so grateful we didn't give up when our world fell apart. We've built a beautiful life together that's worth choosing day after day. Even though I'm not easy to be married to, even though I'm selfish and impetuous, Vic has girded up his loins, gritted his teeth, and stayed the course. We are an interesting pairing, to be sure. But, our names are literally set in stone on Lucy's headstone . . . so . . .

Today is May 29, 2024, our twentieth wedding anniversary. It feels like twenty lifetimes.

BLOG POST: MAY 29, 2008

I don't mean to take away from honoring Lucy. But I think she would want to honor her dad today too. So please bear with me. If you weren't at her funeral or at her bedside in the hospital this week, you missed witnessing some of the world's sweetest miracles.

Vic was one of those miracles to me.

Today is our 4th anniversary. They have been wonderful years. Full of joy and full of trials, but no trial as great as what we are currently experiencing. I once said that I always thought I had married a great man when I chose Vic, then I saw him as a father and I realized I had married a wonderful, rare, and precious man. Well, this past week I have seen yet another man emerge. A man I can scarcely describe. A man so close to God, so full of strength, a man with so much courage, love, and faith, I know few who exist. That man is Lucy's father. He always will be. He is my husband, my companion, my rock.

As Lucy lay on life support, Vic was given an impression that brought a stillness amid the storm: *"Vic, I will take care of Lucy. You take care of Molly."* In that moment, he was handed a purpose within his heartbreak, one that he has taken on with a love so powerful that it has lifted me through the darkest hours. His strength has been nothing short of miraculous—a miracle meant for me, a miracle meant for us.

I love you, my Vicky Poo. We will never be the same after this experience. We will be more loving, more kind, more caring, more united. What a special marriage. Happy Anniversary.

With all my liver and lungs,
Your eternal wife—Molly

PART THREE

THE CALL

There comes a moment in all of our lives when we feel a pull—
an undeniable call toward something greater than ourselves. It's
a quiet whisper or a deep ache urging us to do something with the
lessons we've learned, to turn our pain into purpose. This is *The Call*.
And answering it is what transforms everything that came before.

For me, *The Call* came in the wake of unimaginable loss. I found
myself standing at a crossroads, unsure of how to move forward, or if
moving forward was even possible. But deep down, I knew the only
way to survive was to allow others to bear witness to my pain. I had
to speak the unspeakable, to let people see me in all my raw,
vulnerable truth. And in doing so, I discovered something
remarkable: connection is the key to healing. By allowing others into
my brokenness, I began to find the pieces of myself again.

This is the part of the journey where we choose whether or not to
accept *The Call*. It's not easy, and it certainly does not come without
fear. But when we embrace vulnerability, when we share our
struggles and allow others to hold space for our pain, we step into a
purpose far greater than we ever imagined. We become part of

something bigger—a web of connection that sustains us, heals us, and reminds us we are never truly alone.

The Call is not just about surviving our darkest moments—it's about choosing to thrive. It's about taking what we've been through and using it to help others heal. It's about answering that pull to share hope, to show others that by being vulnerable and letting themselves be seen, they, too, can find healing through connection.

I choose to accept *The Call*, to share my story, and to reach out to those who feel like they're drowning. My hope is that by reading these pages, you'll feel that same pull toward connection, toward vulnerability, and ultimately, toward healing.

This is the beginning of a greater purpose. It's your story, your call. Will you answer it?

Gently wiping that snot off your face.
Routine. Nothing special. Inconvenient, even.

Now, a longed-for privilege.

Stretching for years in my cocoon to break free
Puncturing the silk threads by accepting:
Accidents happen
Loss is part of life
Death is not the end
It's not my fault

Oh, but to see you grow
To be robbed of the magic of your childhood
A blow beyond measure
The pain made sharper against the backdrop of child 2 and 3

They need you here
Our dynamic splintered by your absence.
Your life silenced far too soon rings mercilessly at a painful
pitch in my ears.

But my only choice is to emerge from the chrysalis
With greater empathy
A kinder, softer heart
A freedom not known to those who haven't suffered the
ultimate loss
Wings so vivid and bright that others are drawn to me
Comforted in my presence
Safe in the arms of my knowing pain

Scars are the body's way of reminding us that we have survived, that we have endured. They are both a testament to the pain we have experienced and a symbol of our resilience. In many ways, my deepest scars are invisible—etched not into my skin but into my soul. Yet, these scars have become the most beautiful part of me, a source of strength and a reminder that, even in the darkest moments, there is a way forward.

I gave the following speech at Abbravanell Hall as the keynote speaker for the Transplant Games of America. It received a standing ovation.

Tonight, I'd like to talk about scars. Some seen, most unseen. I know everyone in this room has them. I want to tell you a little about mine.

Of course, I have the usual scars one accumulates during childhood—a small scar on my upper right eyelid from the gash I probably deserved after falling off the bed and onto the metal bed frame at two years old. I was monkeying around, of course.

Or the scar on my knee I earned in college while midnight rollerblading the streets of Provo and hitting an unforeseen patch of gravel.

I have the small and unseen scars of past unrequited loves and deep disappointments, loneliness, and hurt.

But nothing compares to the scars I live with now: the scars that only those of us who have lost a loved one can understand. Sometimes, we're the only ones who can ever see them or recognize them in others.

Before I tell you too much about how I got my deepest scars, I want to share a quote with you from a book I recently finished, called *Little Bee*. Little Bee is a Nigerian girl who witnessed and survived horrific tragedy in her country, as well as enduring two years inside a British immigration detention center. She implores the reader, "I ask you, right here, to please agree with me that a scar is never ugly. That is what the scar makers want us to think. But you and I, we must make an agreement to defy them. We must see all scars as beauty. Okay? This will be our secret."

The soul-searing pain and opening of my psychological wounds began on a beautiful Sunday in May of 2008. After primping for church and finally making it out the door with my soon-to-be two-year-old daughter, Lucy, we sat restlessly in our pew for as long as we could manage before needing to take her energetic bundle out to the foyer for distraction and consoling.

When we realized she wasn't going to settle down and got her strapped in her car seat to leave, I handed her a small Tupperware of thinly sliced apples. That's when she began to choke. That's when I called for my husband and he administered the Heimlich maneuver. That's when my eyes locked with hers for the last time. That's when friends and medical professionals poured out of the church building to assist us, and eventually the life-flight helicopter landed and whisked her body away.

That's when I knew I would never be the same. The irreversible wounds would become scars I'd carry the rest of my life.

But the deepest cut came when I held my daughter in my arms and the organ recovery team wheeled us down the hallway to the yellow line where I gave my daughter's body away. I knew that scar would be the most beautiful.

I heard later, after Lucy's grandmothers reverently dressed her for the burial, of the long and precise scars on her body where her perfect little organs were removed to save the lives of other scarred and scared souls.

Not only do her recipients share her organs, they share her scars.

For every grieving face I see here tonight, there is another living face out there in the world, sharing the scars of your loved ones.

In seven short weeks I am due to give birth to a little girl, due on Lucy's birthday. Bringing her into the world will be painful and no doubt leave some scarring. But the beauty that comes with this new life will be worth the pain. A healing balm.

I know everyone here tonight has scars, deep wounds that are still very tender and raw . . . still bleeding, even. Others, perhaps, have tightened and hardened over the years, but they are there.

I want you to remember our earlier agreement we made with Little Bee about our scars being beautiful. Sometimes people have to look away because they see too much beauty, and we can't blame them.

So be proud of your scars, and the MORE-THAN-HONORABLE scars left on the bodies of those we love and buried.

THERE WILL BE HEALING. You will experience your own healing balms in your life that will help soothe the sting.

Have faith that your scars will become more elastic, and you will be able to bend and stretch and live your life with greater range of motion, embracing the scars you share with your departed and knowing you hold a beauty, wisdom, perspective, gift, and knowledge that the scarless will never know.

CHAPTER 11

Third Dimension

Driving home from Lucy's funeral and then shuffling into an empty house sent me into an indescribable third dimension of existence. Do those of you with children remember what life was like before having kids? Remember how you had a decent grasp on what it meant to be an adult human existing in the world? You had friendships, family, probably a job, some stressors, some hopes and dreams, and some heartaches. You were learning about love and hard work and how to interact with the world at large. It made sense, in a way. You had your role and understood it to a degree.

But then your child came along and you entered a second dimension you didn't even know existed. The way you saw the entire world dramatically shifted. You mean, every human walking the planet has a MOM? Why doesn't everyone I pass in the grocery store stop and marvel at this person I created? This is insane! This is daunting, hard, amazing, stinky work, this loving and raising a child business. Everything feels different.

Well, when you lose a child, this happens again. But this threshold into the third dimension is even more intense. Instead of marveling at how each of us comes into the world, curious and hopeful that everyone is loved as much as you love your child, you become aware of how much pain and heartache exists in the world.

Instead of wondering why everyone in the store isn't in awe of your newborn child, you wander the aisles like a zombie, wishing everyone knew you were bleeding out, in distress, and close to dying. Just as you wanted others to celebrate the new life in your arms, you want others to somehow acknowledge the crushing weight you are now carrying. How could they just go on as before when the world as I knew it had been obliterated? There were times I wanted to wear a shirt with the words, "Bereaved Mother" printed on it. I needed to be treated with extreme tenderness and care. I felt like a newborn child myself—entirely alone in this new world.

One day, I did what any exhausted and overwhelmed child would do: I climbed into Lucy's crib in the hopes of finding comfort or sleep.

Being small helps. I had done it before, crawled into my daughter's crib. I knew it could hold my weight. Before, it had been to read to my daughter, comfort her, or my favorite pastime of all: make her giggle from the belly of her soul. This time, it was holding more than my body weight, it was holding the universe. I had just buried my firstborn two weeks shy of her second birthday.

Overwhelmed in body and spirit, I hoisted my depleted bag of flesh and bones into the crib I had purchased from a yard sale. My mom and sister had paid for the bedding set from Pottery Barn: a bright pink, yellow, and blue quilted pattern called the "Lucy Set."

I could still smell her on the fitted sheet. Her favorite yellow fleece blanket that she called her "B" was folded in the corner. Her name was written in black sharpie on a piece of masking tape that had been stuck to it to label it at the hospital: "This belongs to Lucy Jackson." My friend Kristin Gardner had made that blanket for Lucy.

It was cheap Walmart fabric with long slits cut around the edges and the strips of fabric tied into small knots. It didn't breathe well, was matted and pilled, and Lucy went everywhere with it.

After a solid ten minutes in the fetal position, my body wracked and shuddered with full body sobs, frightened that this feeling of intense longing and pain would crush and kill me, I suddenly sensed an army of unseen women hovering above and around me. I was audibly pleading for someone to hold me, someone to rescue me, see me, heal me, pour peace over me, give me breath. It sounds crazy, but the energy of wise warrior women surrounded me. The only woman among them I knew for certain was my Grandma Gayle, my mother's mother. The other spirits in the room were more vague—spirits I knew I would get to know in the next life, spirits of women who had crossed the plains, fought in battles, buried children, plowed fields until their hands bled.

I felt them say to me, "We endured the unthinkable. Our struggles were great. We know your pain, we know your grief, we lived through the unimaginable, we were exhausted to our core, but we never gave up hope. We are holding you." I like to think Abigail Adams was among them. I was actually jealous of Abigail while I was dating my husband because he talked about her so much. That's correct, I was jealous of a dead woman. But I knew she was a woman of depth who faced intense trials with grace.

In that moment, I could feel these beautiful, soft, strong women extend an invitation: "Do you want to be counted among us? Do you want to be a woman of strength and courage? We will show you how and we will not abandon you. We have done it and so can you."

Clearly, in my mind's eye, I could see and feel decades of trauma from these women combined with the determination to overcome the trauma. Their stories cradled me. With what felt like gallons of snot running down my face, I accepted the invitation into my heart. I would rise to the challenge like they had. I would absorb my story of loss into my DNA, and I would use it to bolster my heart, not tamper it. I would show others—especially myself—that healing is possible. This experience was my first taste of healing through connection.

I don't remember getting out of the crib, but I'll never forget what happened while I was in it.

CHAPTER 12

Speak the Unspeakable

It was 2008, and I had started a family blog just a few months before Lucy's death. Now, bereft and alone in our little condo, I began to spill my heart and mind onto the pages of our blog. I shared the ugly, the brutal, the beautiful, and the mundane of a mom's life torn apart by the reality of a world that has no compunction about our devastations and no restraint in knocking us down.

The loss of a child is, thankfully, more and more rare in this world, but the reality of loss and grief is something we all know. As I wrote through my grief, I found people who knew the pain of losing a child and others whose hearts, though faced with different losses, nonetheless resonated with my experience. Sometimes, my words scared my relatively reserved, "don't let your emotions control you; let's keep a positive face" husband. Sometimes my words scared me too. Life can be painful. Devastatingly painful.

But because I had the courage to speak my unspeakable, I experienced connections deeper than I'd ever known.

Strangers from the internet flooded us with love, gifts, and words of wisdom and comfort. People from church shared stories of losing their brother, their niece, their mom.

I always knew humanity was good, but this tragedy magnified its goodness. Yes, some people said stupid, insensitive things, but by and large the love, compassion, and incredible acts of charity we received were as astounding as our pain. This is the gift of speaking the unspeakable.

My connections helped me feel vulnerable enough to speak—to let people into the darkest corners of my grief—which in turn gave others permission to speak their unspeakable to me. My worldview dramatically shifted. I learned how much pain and loss everyone is experiencing, has experienced, or will experience. Pain is a powerful connector.

My connections with others saved my life when my daughter lost hers.

Brené Brown defines connection as, "the energy that exists between people when they feel seen, heard, and valued; when they can give and receive without judgment; and when they derive sustenance and strength from the relationship" (from *The Gifts of Imperfection: Let Go of Who You Think You're Supposed to Be and Embrace Who You Are*).

Indeed, the people willing to not turn away but to truly see and value and hear my heartbreak were like sustenance to my soul. I had to know we could survive this. Carrying a pain this heavy alone was not an option.

True, no one can take away your pain, but they can ease it. Sometimes simply by acknowledging it, pain eases. Speaking it out loud gives it breathing room.

At the right time, in the right way, in the safety of trusted relationships, we must find the courage to speak the unspeakable. In my experience, it is the most powerful tool for connection.

But this isn't about airing dirty laundry or violently unloading our emotional baggage on others. Nor is it an invitation to complain endlessly about life's struggles. Instead, it's a practice of bravery, vulnerability, and trust. Expressing what feels embarrassing, scary, or hidden deep in our hearts—even if it's something positive like a compliment, admiration, or a secret hope—is how we strengthen the most valuable commodity we have in life: connection.

The courage to speak my unspeakable and cultivate authentic connection is the main reason I survived such an enormous loss.

And now, because I have shared my unspeakable with you, we are connected. And it is an honor. Thank you for allowing me to speak my daughter's name.

Applying "Speak the Unspeakable" in a Professional Setting

While the idea of speaking the unspeakable may seem deeply personal, its power extends far beyond our private lives. In the professional world, fostering a culture where employees feel safe to express their unspeakable truths—whether it's a personal struggle, an idea that challenges the status quo, or a fear of failure—can transform a workplace. This vulnerability, when met with compassion and understanding, strengthens teams and builds trust.

For leaders, this begins with modeling the behavior themselves. When those in leadership positions demonstrate that it's OK to share challenges and admit when they don't have all the answers, they create an environment where others feel safe to do the same. Authentic connection isn't just a personal tool, it's a leadership strategy. Employees who feel seen, heard, and valued are more engaged, innovative, and loyal.

Creating this culture requires more than an open-door policy. It means actively listening and responding with empathy when someone speaks their unspeakable. It's not about solving every problem or providing immediate answers; sometimes, it's simply about holding space for people to express themselves without being judged. Compassionate listening can be transformative, and in many cases, it's what fosters connection, creativity, and resilience within a team.

When leaders embrace vulnerability and foster this culture, employees are more likely to speak up when they need help, share new ideas, and contribute to an environment where everyone feels supported. This isn't just good for employee morale—it's essential for long-term business success. Companies that prioritize authentic connection often find that their teams are more adaptable, collaborative, and innovative. Employees are empowered to take risks, knowing that even if they fail, they won't be met with criticism but with understanding and support.

In this way, the professional world benefits from the same principle that guides personal healing: speaking the unspeakable fosters authentic connection, and that connection becomes the foundation of a thriving, resilient organization.

CHAPTER 13

Use your
Gifts to be a Gift

I want you to picture a woman with shoulder-length blonde hair—
and it's BIG. No, bigger. Now, just go a little bit bigger than that.
Then, get out your ratting comb and back-comb it a few inches. Add
some hairspray—Aquanet, preferably. Next, add a Bump It (please
tell me some of you remember those hair contraptions from the '90s).
For good measure, let's add another two inches of volume. Can you
picture it? Yes, her hair is just as big and blonde as your brain is
picturing.

This woman's name is Jennie. Jennie is one of EIGHT children.
FIVE of Jennie's siblings were born with a very rare genetic disorder
called Wolfram syndrome. As the oldest child, Jennie watched as her
parents cared for these special children. In a way, Wolfram syndrome
is a bit like childhood ALS. Jennie helped care for, love, and bury all
five of these siblings.

When my little Lucy was in the hospital for those four sacred,
gutting days, Jennie showed up on day three with a perfect little white
burial dress she had sewn. It was Lucy's exact size. She didn't ask if

we wanted her to make it. We weren't even sure at that point what the final outcome of the situation would be. But Jennie knew. And she knew exactly what to do—from the burial dress to the balloons and flowers at the funeral to the luncheon after the funeral—because she had done this five times before.

Jennie was our neighbor as well as our ward's Relief Society president—that's Mormon lingo for the leader of our church's women's organization. I always thought she was a sweet, kind, hardworking lady. But before Lucy's accident, I had no idea about her life story and experiences.

Regardless of your religious orientation or personal beliefs, I think much of the world knows the story surrounding the birth of Christ. In reference to this widely celebrated occasion, an LDS apostle named Neal A. Maxwell once said, "Recall the new star that announced the birth at Bethlehem? It was in its precise orbit long before it so shone. We are likewise placed in human orbits to illuminate" (from "Encircled in the Arms of His Love," October 5, 2002).

No quote or concept could come closer to describing the way Jennie appeared in our life. She was placed in a precise orbit to illuminate us in the darkness of our despair. She gently shone at the exact time we needed her. All of the gifts that Jennie had acquired throughout her life—her sewing skills, her woodworking skills, her talents as a designer (there is nothing this woman can't do . . . she built her own house), her emotional capacity and intimacy with death, her cooking—were all given as gifts to Vic and me.

Every year on Lucy's birthday she ties bright pink ribbons on the flowering crabapple tree in Pinebrook Park that my castmates from *Peter Pan* planted in honor of Lucy. Not only that, she saved part of the fabric from Lucy's burial dress *just in case* I had another little girl so that she could sew a blessing dress for her.

As for her hair? I figured out why it's so big and so blond. I honestly had this revelation and laughed at first. And then I cried because I swear it's true, and I told her so.

The reason she teases her hair so big and bleaches it so blonde is that she has to hide her halo.

Use YOUR gifts to be a gift. Listen to me: it doesn't matter what they are. They don't have to be bright and shiny talents. You have a gift with numbers and spreadsheets? YOU'RE MY SAVIOR. I see a spreadsheet and my brain shuts DOWN. Cooking? Cleaning? The gift of understanding technology? Party planning? A bladder of steel? The gift of being able to sleep easily? (I'd kill for that!) Oh! What about the gift of patience with children? You daycare workers and teachers out there . . . ABSOLUTE GIFTS FROM GOD and doing what is certainly not my calling.

Not only does using your gifts to bless others create connection, it's the reason you have them in the first place. It's how we create the interconnected web of human creativity, beauty, and a literal strong safety net for when the inevitable happens. What's the inevitable? Death. Hard times. Heartache. Health problems. Stress. The ridiculousness of being mortal.

Take a moment and think about your gifts. Write them down. I know someone reading this has an insanely keen and wicked sense of humor. You lighten up difficult situations and bring people to tears with laughter. Write that down.

Someone else is the best ski teacher in the Rocky Mountain West. You're killing it. You're connecting with your students and giving them skills that will lead to lifelong adventures in majestic mountains.

And you, over there in the corner, you're the best at interior design. Yep. Yes, you are. You give people a beautiful, peaceful, sacred space to lay their head down at night. It matters.

Chef, host, bike mechanic, sales person, bricklayer, student, doctor, lobbyist, house cleaner, architect, tattoo artist—WE NEED YOUR GIFTS. You matter. Thank you for making the world go round and using your gifts to be a gift to others. If you're feeling lost in your story and down about your life, go drop your literal and figurative gift at someone's feet. You'll make a new friend and a new reason to carry on one more blasted day.

As Tara Mohr teaches in her book, *Playing Big* (which my therapist insisted I read after years of hearing me complain about how to balance the warring sides of myself), "We are each a cell in the larger body of human community. We are meant to live and work in circles, to make our contribution to the whole." Talk about VALUE!

Jennie showed me that grief is sacred work. Jennie showed me that although the orbit I've been placed in may not make sense right now, I will be able to shine on others in their exact moment of need. They can look to me for guidance. My unique light can illuminate their path.

It's been sixteen years since Lucy died. I still can't fly, but I am dancing again.

Applying "Use Your Gifts to Be a Gift" in a Professional Setting

The idea of using your gifts to be a gift extends far beyond personal relationships. In the professional world, leaders have a unique opportunity—and responsibility—to recognize and cultivate the talents of their team members. A thriving workplace isn't just about assigning tasks that fit a job description, it's about identifying the unique gifts employees bring, even if those gifts don't seem directly related to the employee's role.

When leaders take the time to truly see their employees—to notice their hidden skills, passions, and strengths—they create a culture where people feel valued for who they are, not just what they do. This, in turn, builds a sense of belonging, trust, and loyalty within the team.

Incorporating employees' unique gifts into the fabric of a company starts with noticing and acknowledging them. Perhaps you have an employee whose knack for storytelling could improve how you pitch to clients, or a team member with a talent for photography who could enhance the visual aspects of your brand. Maybe someone has an exceptional ability to make others feel heard and supported— an invaluable skill for improving team morale. Leaders who tap into these gifts and integrate them into the workplace create opportunities for employees to shine, feel fulfilled, and contribute in ways that go beyond their job titles.

At its core, this approach fosters connection. When employees feel seen for their true talents and are encouraged to use them to benefit the company, they are more likely to be engaged, motivated, and loyal. They feel like they are contributing to something greater than themselves and that their unique light is illuminating the path forward for the whole team.

This isn't just good for team morale, it's good for business. When employees are given the space to bring their whole selves to work, creativity and innovation flourish. Each person's gifts combine to form a powerful, interconnected web of strengths that can help the company weather challenges, adapt to change, and drive success.

Leaders can foster this environment by creating opportunities for employees to share their gifts. This could be through collaborative projects that encourage cross-functional talents, mentorship programs that allow people to teach others what they know, or even company-wide celebrations that highlight individuals' unique contributions.

It's also about listening. Leaders should ask questions that go beyond the usual performance reviews:

What are you passionate about?

What do you enjoy doing outside of work?

What skills do you have that we haven't yet tapped into?

These conversations open the door for employees to share their unsung talents and for leaders to find ways to harness those talents within the organization.

In the corporate world, as in life, using your gifts to be a gift builds connection, creates meaning, and makes both the workplace and the world a better place. By applying this tool, leaders create a culture where everyone feels valued, seen, and motivated to contribute their unique strengths to the collective success of the team.

CHAPTER 14

Don't Try to Prove Yourself, Just Try to BE Yourself

If you're an Instagram enthusiast like me, you might remember when Instagram introduced the "Stories" feature. If that sentence means nothing to you, congratulations on living in the real world, free from the grip of social media. I applaud you. It might also mean you're, well . . . older . . . and that's perfectly OK.

For the record, it was August of 2016 when "Stories" were introduced.

For those unfamiliar, an Instagram Story is a post or video that disappears after 24 hours. It's a fleeting moment, something you want to share without having it permanently on your page. The feature creates urgency, encouraging followers to check back regularly so they don't miss that day's content. It mimics the ephemerality of real-life interactions—here one moment, gone the next.

I'll never forget the day a fluffy- and curly-haired blonde beauty appeared on my screen wearing a rainbow-striped robe while dancing in her kitchen. There she was—no makeup, no filter, no script—just raw and real. She spoke directly to the camera, her raspy voice full of joy. I felt as though I were sitting at her kitchen counter, hearing about her chaotic morning.

Her authenticity stopped me in my tracks. Wait, you can just *be* yourself on social media? I had shared raw and heartfelt words online before—written through my blog—and I prided myself on being my genuine self. But putting my unfiltered self out there in front of a camera for the whole world to see? In a bathrobe? Laughing and chatting aimlessly? I hadn't realized that was even an option. Up until then, I had only seen carefully posed photos, cute little quotes, filtered videos, and dogs in bowties. But this woman—this was a real human being: a frazzled, dancing mom in her kitchen, no pretenses.

Her name was Brooke White. She was a finalist on *American Idol* in 2008—*the year my daughter died.* Memorial Day weekend, when Lucy passed, was the same weekend as the *Idol* finale. I'll never forget sitting in the parents' waiting room at Primary Children's Hospital, sobbing, unable to eat, as the final episode aired. While David Archuleta and David Cook stood on stage singing their hearts out in front of millions, my daughter was down the hall on life support. I was a 105-pound shell of a human watching two strangers live their dreams while mine was withering in the darkest of places. The contrast was unbearable.

Years later, after I had embraced my inner "online mother of madness," I became friends with Brooke. I realized the irony—her moment of fame coinciding with my greatest loss. Yet it was her simple act of being herself that showed me a new path. Brooke taught me that **we can only connect to what is real.** Let that sink in.

We can only connect to what is real.

If you want to make an impact, you have to be authentic. Sure, you may need to keep your crazy in check sometimes (as the classic movie *Girls Just Want to Have Fun* reminds us, "There's a time and a place for Calypso music"), but being genuine is nonnegotiable.

When I discovered the magic of being my goofy, weird, wonderful self online, a whole new world opened up to me. You mean to tell me there's a free platform where entertainers at heart can post their "home videos" and broadcast them to the masses? Sign me up for my one-woman *SNL* show *immediately*.

And so began my adventures of filming myself dancing in the kitchen, on mountain trails, and even in the break room at the Park City Library where I worked for a year as the adult assistant librarian. (I love libraries. In fact, I'm sitting in the Jackson Hole Library as I write this.) It was an interesting job, though I was dying inside as I was surrounded by books that weren't mine. I vowed that the next time I entered the Park City Library it would be for an author event featuring me and my book baby. But I digress.

After posting one of my first kitchen dance videos, a college friend messaged me. Janique—some of you might know her as Alexis from @letstalksis—had seen me being a fool online. She messaged me, "My kids and I are cuddled on the couch watching you be ridiculous. We love it!"

I was so surprised and touched that being my goofy self brought my friend and her kids together for a moment of laughter. That sparked an idea I couldn't ignore. I replied, "I'm going to do another stupid dance and dedicate it to you and your kids. Make sure they see it!"

Another shimmy and moonwalk later, I received a reply from Janique: "We are smiling like idiots. My kids loved it!"

And with that, the "Positive Pants Dance" was born.

Every Thursday for about seven years, I held a virtual dance party in my kitchen. I asked my followers to share something positive that happened to them, and I'd dedicate a dance to them in my Instagram stories. From successful garden crops to landing jobs after months of unemployment, my kitchen became a celebration of life's little victories.

There is no denying the energy of authenticity. You know it when you see it. You can feel it instantly.

This can be tricky in work settings, where we often feel the need to be on our best behavior. But being yourself doesn't mean sacrificing professionalism; it means showing up with your unique energy, creativity, and personality. By letting go of who we think we're supposed to be, we give ourselves—and others—permission to be who we all really are. In a world full of constraints and pressures, this authenticity is one less burden to carry.

Yes, my Instagram following grew like my publisher wanted it to, but it didn't grow because I was perfectly curated. It grew because I showed up real, sharing everything from adventures in Europe to tears over Lucy, from milk dripping through my ceiling to fears about money and purpose. I've made real-life friends, booked speaking gigs, connected with other grieving moms, been a podcast guest, and received generous gifts . . . all because I chose to *be* myself instead of trying to prove myself. **You cannot get the connection you seek if you are putting forth a false self.**

Isn't it a miracle that I can dance again? That I can feel joy again? That we are all connected in so many ways? These are some of the many miracles I never thought possible.

Brooke showed me that authenticity is the key to connection. She gave me permission to be myself in a world obsessed with curation.

Although I had blogged through my grief for years after Lucy's death, this new platform allowed me to connect in ways I hadn't before. Social media will never replace in-person connection, but it can help remind us that, beneath the filters and captions, we're all human. We all struggle. As the saying by Arlan Hamilton goes, **"Be yourself, so the people looking for you can find you"** (from *It's About Damn Time*).

From Brooke, I learned that I didn't have to give up my silly side just because I am a grieving mother. We all contain **ANDs**. I am a grieving mom AND a comedian. I am a mom AND an individual. I am hopeful AND broken. Most importantly, I am not everyone's cup of tea AND I am exactly the hot drink someone else has been craving.

Leaders, parents, teachers, and friends—cultivate an environment where people feel safe to be themselves. It increases job satisfaction and retention, and leads to deeper engagement. When people feel safe to be authentic, they'll show you their best selves. They'll form meaningful connections, find friends, and unlock their true potential.

As Shauna Niequist writes, **"People aren't longing to be impressed; they are longing to feel like they're home. If you create a space full of love and character and creativity and soul, they'll take off their shoes and curl up with gratitude and rest, no matter how small, no matter how undone, no matter how odd"** (from *Bread and Wine: A Love Letter to Life around the Table, with Recipes*).

If a striped-robe-wearing, kitchen-dancing, joyful stranger can make me feel at home, imagine what you can do for the souls of the people in your circle.

Applying "Don't Try to Prove Yourself, Just Try to BE Yourself" in a Professional Setting

In a professional environment, it can feel like the pressure to *prove* ourselves is constant. We set goals, we strive for promotions, we want to be recognized for our hard work—and often, this creates a culture of self-promotion and competition. But the truth is, focusing solely on proving yourself, rather than *being yourself*, can lead to burnout, frustration, and inauthentic connections. You can still meet your goals and show your value by being the best version of yourself rather than an artificial version designed to impress.

The key difference between proving yourself and being yourself at work is the mindset shift. When you focus on proving yourself, you tend to overemphasize your accomplishments, hide your vulnerabilities, and present a version of yourself that you think others want to see. You make it about external validation—trying to fit into a mold that may not feel natural. But when you approach your work by being yourself, you focus on your strengths, your passion, and your unique way of contributing. You're not striving to be seen as perfect or flawless but as capable, creative, and committed.

Being yourself doesn't mean abandoning professionalism or disregarding goals—it means showing up as the authentic, best version of you. You can still be driven, ambitious, and focused on results, but when you align those goals with your true self, you tap into a deeper source of motivation and creativity. You're not proving your worth, you're embodying it.

Ultimately, your authenticity is your strength. Trying to prove yourself by pretending to be something you're not is unsustainable. But when you allow yourself to be authentic, you build lasting connections, strengthen your relationships at work, and even enhance your performance. Authenticity is magnetic: people gravitate toward those who are genuine because it fosters trust and respect.

So, yes, we all have goals to meet. Yes, there are times we need to advocate for our growth, negotiate for raises, and prove that we deserve that next step. But we don't have to do it by wearing a mask. **We can do it by being our best, most authentic selves.**

When you approach work in this way, you're no longer just *proving* you're worthy of success—you're *being* worthy of it.

CHAPTER 15

Gratitude Chain

Discovering and coining the term for this next connection tool fills me with indescribable delight. It's extremely accessible, universal, low stakes, *and* it's highly effective. I'm stoked to be sharing it with your brain and eyeballs right now!

The genesis of this powerful concept took place on a gorgeous and thrill-inducing mountain bike trail in Park City.

About a decade ago, we purchased a used mountain bike from Facebook Marketplace for $500. That was a lot of money for us then (honestly, it still is). It was light blue and it was some brand that I can't remember and is no longer made. But the best part about it is that it had full suspension. SO FANCY and so necessary if you want to be considered a real Parkite and a "real" mountain biker.

With the help of my friend Sherri Swing, I learned the basics of the sport and would set out as often as possible to explore the world-class trails my city has to offer.

To put my new skills to the test, one day I invited my friend Monica—to whom I've given the award of "Best Listener on the Face of the Earth"—to go biking with me. Even though Monica and I have had NUMEROUS misadventures together—locking my keys in my car when we went skiing; convincing her to "just try" a particular trail which led to a majorly technical downhill jumpy, twisty, berm situation, and SHE WAS ESSENTIALLY ON A TEN SPEED (I am undulating with laughter just thinking about it)—she agreed to come with me.

On this particular day, she borrowed her husband's mountain bike and joined me near the Utah Olympic Park to ooh and aah at the views, get a great workout, and continue the conversion process of becoming a real mountain biker. (There is real fear of losing your Park City citizenship if you don't mountain bike and ski.)

After a hot and steady climb, a few missed turns, and a consultation or two of the trail map, we reached the glorious peak of the mountain with its breathtaking views. That's when the fun part began: over three miles of whoop-de-dos and up-and-downs and little jumps and flowing turns (these are technical terms only real mountain bikers will know).

Granted, I *had* taken my Adderall that day, but nonetheless, I was in the ZONE. I felt extremely alive and present. The cool mountain air gloriously filled my lungs with each deep breath. Music from my airpods streaming into my ears, I proceeded to make my spirited descent.

Moments like this are the living example of my favorite quote, which bears repeating: "The cavity which suffering carves into our souls will one day also be the receptacle of joy."

This wasn't just another bike ride for me on another random summer day. This was a wounded woman filled with deep joy after years of drilling pain.

With my strong body, a loving friend trailing behind me, and blood pumping happily through my veins, I began to speak my gratitude out loud.

"I'm so grateful for this garage-sale bike!"

"I'm so grateful for the factory that made these thick tires and the people who work there!" (My grandmother had worked in a rubber-tire factory and developed emphysema. I thought of her and the difficult life she tried to live with grace.)

"I'm so grateful for the people who built and maintain these trails!"

"I'm so grateful I have fuel from food in my body that gives me the energy to experience this!"

"I'm so grateful for the farmers who grew the food!"

"I'm so grateful for the truck drivers who haul the food hundreds of miles to the grocery store."

"I'm so grateful to the grocers who unload the trucks with their bare hands so I can purchase the food."

"I'm so grateful to Vic for providing a good life for our family. I'm so grateful he gets out of bed every morning and goes to work despite his depression and grief. I'm grateful he went to law school so he could build a good career. I'm so grateful to his parents for raising a good, kind man. I'm grateful to his law professors. Grateful for the men and women who built the Pepperdine campus where he studied. Grateful for the investors and architects. Grateful I moved to LA where I was able to meet him."

ON AND ON AND ON.

THIS is the gratitude chain—the great "GC," I just decided to call it while typing. (Do we think it'll become a thing? Probably not. As

Regina George says to Gretchen Weiners in *Mean Girls*, "Stop trying to make *fetch* happen.")

Talk about connection! The gratitude chain quickly and easily shifts us into a mindset of belonging, of knowing we all play a part in the chain of humanity. The more often we put this tool into practice, the more we will feel part of something greater than ourselves. It nourishes our sense of belonging and increases our capacity to heal and our desire to contribute.

But the best news is that we can do this anytime, anywhere, with anything or anyone—be it an object (my blasted cell phone that I love/hate), a person (my incredible vestibular therapist who has saved me from complete hopelessness and mental chaos during two nervous system breakdowns over the course of five years), or a place (the beautiful cemetery in Salt Lake City where our Lucy is buried).

Right now, I want you to think of something you are grateful for.

What's an obvious and immediate connection to it?

Go further.

Add on another chain.

Every good thing, even in the midst of tragedy, can be linked to another good thing. For me, this practice instills a sense of groundedness—a reminder that I am not drifting through life alone but am held by a web of human connection.

You may wonder, "But Molly, how could I apply this in the face of a tragedy? How can I possibly find gratitude in *that*?" It's not easy. But taking the first step by creating a gratitude chain, even in the darkest times, opens the door to healing. It allows us to find small moments of grace in our heartache. And when life is going well, it deepens and magnifies our joy.

Our society often fixates on gratitude for material things (cue the hashtag, #BLESSED), but the real, life-changing gratitude lies in our connections to people.

Applying the "Gratitude Chain" in a Professional Setting

The beauty of the gratitude chain is that it isn't limited to our personal lives. In fact, applying this tool in a professional setting can radically shift how we view our work, our colleagues, and the larger systems that enable us to do what we do. Gratitude is a powerful force in fostering connection, and the more we consciously practice it in our work environments, the more we cultivate appreciation, collaboration, and engagement.

Here's a simple exercise to demonstrate how to use the gratitude chain at work:

Let's start with something as ordinary as a *laptop*—a tool many of us use daily. At first glance, it might seem like an impersonal object, just a piece of technology that enables you to get your work done. But when you practice the gratitude chain, you begin to see the interconnected web of people, skills, and efforts that make that object valuable.

1. **Start with the object itself**: "I'm grateful for this laptop that allows me to work remotely, communicate with my team, and stay productive."

2. **Link it to the next connection**: "I'm grateful to the engineers and designers who created this laptop, who spent years mastering their craft to develop this technology."

3. **Dig deeper**: "I'm grateful to the factory workers who assembled the parts and the shipping teams who transported the laptops to stores and warehouses."

4. **Extend the connection**: "I'm grateful for the IT department at my company, who set up my laptop and ensure everything runs smoothly, allowing me to focus on my work."

5. **Bring it back to your colleagues**: "I'm grateful for my team members who communicate with me through this laptop, collaborate on projects, and help solve problems every day."

By the end of this gratitude chain, what started as a seemingly simple appreciation for an object becomes a deep recognition of the human efforts, expertise, and relationships that contribute to your success at work. This exercise helps you connect the dots between the tools you rely on and the people who make those tools—and your job—possible.

Practical Application: Try this exercise at the beginning of your workday. Choose an object or process at your workplace—something that might otherwise feel mundane—and create a gratitude chain around it. Start with the object, connect it to the people who designed, made, or maintain it, and then link it to your colleagues or others who benefit from it.

You can even take this practice a step further by expressing your gratitude directly. If you realize how important the IT team is to your workflow, consider sending them a note of appreciation. If you recognize how your colleagues contribute to your success, share that gratitude with them. When people feel seen and appreciated, it strengthens the professional relationships that are at the heart of a thriving workplace.

By regularly practicing the gratitude chain in a professional setting, you not only cultivate a deeper sense of appreciation but you also create stronger connections with the people you work with. Gratitude, when expressed, leads to greater collaboration, higher morale, and a more positive work environment.

CHAPTER 16

Common Denominator

At a recent National Speakers Association event, I found myself instantly connecting with the firecracker standing next to me. She smelled incredible, had on a fabulous blazer, and was practically radiating with an energy that was both magnetic and spicy. A few snarky comments later, we were instant friends.

Within minutes, we were exchanging life stories in bullet points and cracking each other up. She filled me in on all the dirty details—where I could buy her exact blazer, perfume, and lotion—you know, the important things! She also shared that she's a single mom, working hard to provide for her son while chasing her dreams, inspiring others, and navigating the chaos of life. Before long, we exchanged social media handles and promised to stay in touch, all before being asked to take our seats for the meeting.

Our seats were on opposite sides of the room (our purses and water bottles had claimed our places long before our banter began), but we kept messaging each other on Instagram, making each other laugh with our sarcastic commentary on the event.

At some point, I decided I should probably start paying attention to the actual content of the meeting. As I exited our conversation, I glanced at her Instagram profile. And there it was—right on her main page—a proud endorsement of a certain political candidate, one I was definitely *not* a fan of.

For a split second, I thought, "Wait, *her*? Did I just hit it off with someone who supports *that* person?" My initial reaction was one of mild shock, but it quickly gave way to something much more interesting: *delight*. I was thrilled, actually. Here was living proof of one of my most deeply held beliefs: the opposite of hate isn't love—it's connection.

If I had stumbled upon her profile without having met her, I probably would have rolled my eyes and moved right along. But because we connected in real life first, we set aside all the usual judgments and assumptions. We met as two people, two hearts, two stories, and in that space, our differences didn't drive us apart—they enriched our connection. I found myself appreciating her even more because we *didn't* see eye to eye.

This, I realized, is the power of conscious connection. It liberates us from the need to persuade, manipulate, or convince someone to see things our way. It frees us from the wasted energy of wishing people were different—whether it's our partners, neighbors, leaders, or even our children. We don't have to love or believe what they believe, we just have to commit to connecting on common ground.

That's the secret: finding a common denominator is about realizing that no matter how different someone seems, you always share something. Your nosy neighbor? I bet they love chocolate as much as you do. That adorable comedian Nate Bargatze? I'm sure even your weirdest family members are fans. Connect with them over Nate.

Connection doesn't always need to be deep, but its effects are always profound. The greatest disservice we can do to ourselves is to believe we're "other," that we're alone in this mess called humanity.

Here's what's insanely beautiful: every single time I meet someone who has lost a child, I feel an immediate, profound, and real connection that breaks down all barriers. There's no question of whether they're "deserving" of my love, no snap judgments of whether we're "alike enough" to engage. Always, there are instant hugs, often accompanied by immediate tears. It's one of the many gifts Lucy gave us—this bond with others who have experienced unimaginable loss.

Talk about a common denominator.

This is why we have grief support groups, AA meetings, and postpartum support groups. A shared experience instantly puts us at ease. But here's the real secret: our ultimate common denominator is our humanity. Sure, it helps to get more specific, but at the core we're all the same. We're all just trying to get through this messy, beautiful life. We all need to be seen, heard, and valued.

It's not that we think we're different from others—we think we're *separate*. We aren't. Covid taught us that. See also: gratitude chain.

Right now, I'm sitting in a Barnes & Noble in the Sugarhouse neighborhood of Salt Lake City. To my left there are seven people. To my right, four more. I guarantee I have something in common with every single one of them.

Maybe one of them is also writing a book. Maybe someone else has experienced grief, or loves hiking, or finds solace in chocolate ice cream on hard days. Maybe someone has had their heart broken, or maybe someone is just trying to figure out what comes next in life.

Applying the "Common Denominator" in a Professional Setting

In the workplace, it's inevitable that we'll encounter colleagues, bosses, or clients with whom we don't immediately click—or worse, who challenge our patience. It's easy to fall into the trap of focusing on differences, especially in high-pressure environments where deadlines, stress, and personalities collide. But this is where the common denominator practice can be invaluable. Instead of focusing on what separates us, we can deliberately seek out shared experiences, interests, or values that form a bridge between us and those we struggle to connect with.

Here are some ways to apply the common denominator with various people in your professional setting:

1. **With difficult clients**: When dealing with a challenging client, it's easy to fixate on the frustrations—unreasonable demands, communication barriers, or differing priorities. Instead, try to shift your focus to finding something you have in common. Maybe they're passionate about a particular cause or have a shared hobby that you discover in conversation. Ask them about their interests beyond the work project at hand. Even finding out they love a certain type of coffee or follow the same sports team can soften the interaction and create a more personal connection, leading to more productive and cooperative working relationships.

   Example: A client keeps changing the scope of a project, making your work feel impossible. Instead of focusing on your frustration, take a moment to ask about their weekend plans or discuss a recent headline you both saw. You might discover they're overwhelmed by personal commitments or share a common passion for hiking. By finding a shared interest, you humanize the relationship, making it easier to navigate the professional challenges together.

2. **With coworkers**: We don't get to choose our coworkers, and sometimes personalities clash. The common denominator tool can help break down those barriers by focusing on what you *do* share, rather than what sets you apart. Take time to learn about their hobbies, families, or career paths. Even something as simple as sharing a laugh over the same TV show can be a starting point for deeper, more collaborative relationships.

   Example: You've got a coworker whose communication style drives you nuts—they're short in emails, never greet you in the morning, and seem indifferent in meetings. Rather than assuming they dislike you or are difficult by nature, try finding a point of connection. Maybe they're introverted, or maybe they just have a lot on their plate. Ask about something outside of work, like what they do on the weekends. You may discover a shared interest, like a favorite band or similar family background, which can help soften their edges in your eyes and make your working relationship easier.

3. **With your boss**: Sometimes, the distance between you and your boss can feel insurmountable, especially if they have a very different leadership style or vision. But bosses are people, too, and finding a shared denominator can change the dynamic entirely. By looking for common ground—whether it's a shared value, a similar career trajectory, or a love for a particular sport—you can start building rapport. When they feel you understand and respect them as a person, your relationship becomes more fluid, and communication improves.

Example: You're struggling to connect with your boss, who seems hyper-focused on results and less interested in the people behind them. During a casual conversation, you find out they're passionate about travel, just like you. Suddenly, you have something to chat about in the elevator or over lunch. Now, when you approach them with work-related issues, the connection you've built through shared interests makes it easier to have productive, candid conversations.

Here are practical steps for using the common denominator at work

1. **Ask questions**. Be curious about the people you work with, even those who frustrate you. Ask them about their hobbies, what they did over the weekend, or what got them into their line of work. These conversations often reveal shared experiences or interests that can make your professional interactions more enjoyable.

2. **Observe.** Pay attention to details. Maybe a coworker wears a sports jersey, drinks a certain brand of coffee, or talks about a favorite movie. Use these observations as conversation starters to find common ground and build rapport.

3. **Look for shared values**: Even if you have little in common personally, focus on professional values you share. Maybe you both care deeply about quality work or are passionate about a particular cause related to your industry. Focusing on what you both care about can shift the tone of your relationship.

4. **Practice empathy**. Instead of writing off someone whose behavior irritates you, ask yourself what might be driving that

behavior. Are they stressed, overwhelmed, or struggling with something outside of work? Understanding their circumstances can help you find a point of connection and shift your perspective.

The Power of Connection in the Workplace

Finding common ground, even with difficult people, transforms professional relationships. It softens friction, reduces stress, and increases collaboration. When we recognize that, despite our differences, we share common experiences and values, we start to see our colleagues, clients, and bosses as allies rather than obstacles.

Building these connections doesn't mean you have to agree with everything or ignore your frustrations. Instead, it's about realizing that we're all human and have more in common than we might think. In the end, the workplace thrives on relationships, and the stronger those relationships are, the more successful and fulfilling your professional life will be.

CHAPTER 17

Momentary Magic

Woke thinking about Lucy . . . came across this quote so thought I would share.

Time is too slow for those who wait, too swift for those who fear, too long for those who grieve, too short for those who rejoice, but for those who love, time is eternity. ~Henry Van Dyke

It is better for you to ponder these words than for me to give my explanation. But know that I Love You!

Your Friend,
Justin K

I met Justin Kinnaird in 1997 at Ricks College (now BYU-Idaho) on the first day of school. We were both auditioning for my dad's performing group, Showtime Company. After the auditions, Justin approached me and asked if I felt like chatting while walking to his apartment. I still remember what I was wearing: black dance pants, black jazz shoes, and a burnt orange Banana Republic sweatshirt that I had borrowed from a high school friend.

As we walked, he opened up to me about his brother who had recently had surgery and some family friends of his who had just passed away in a car accident. He was so honest, so open, so sincere, so real. His kind and vulnerable ways really struck me. It was the first time I ever remember having a conversation with someone of the opposite sex where I didn't feel uncomfortable, self-conscious, or like I couldn't be myself (a pretty big deal for a nineteen-year-old . . . at least for me).

I left his apartment feeling like a different person. Honestly. In that one walk, that one conversation, I felt a whole new world open up to me: a world where people are real and honest, where they communicate with heartfelt words. There was no flirting, no awkwardness, no pretense . . . just two human beings with beautiful souls enjoying being in the presence of each other. I had experienced this with my girlfriends, but never with a guy.

We both ended up making the performing group and spent the entire year together—singing, dancing, rehearsing, walking to classes together, studying, driving around in his old little gray car, and laughing our heads off. We took trips to Salmon, Idaho and swam in the hot springs, went sledding, hung out with his marvelous parents, and stayed up late talking about life. With our friend Paul we headed to San Francisco to play at the beaches, go shopping, and do some exploring. At the end of that year, we toured together for an entire month with the rest of our performing group. It was heaven.

After college we kept in touch . . . always. We had the same sense of humor and would leave each other the funniest voicemails. We always talked about recording our voicemails into one big album and making an NPR story out of them. They were hilarious. So many different voices and characters were born in those voicemails.

Every guy I dated was compared to Justin. In fact, when Vic and I were talking about getting married, Vic tells me I walked over to the phone, called Justin and asked him if he thought the two of us would ever get married. When he told me, "no," I hung up and was able to tell Vic that we could go ahead and get married. Oh, Molly. The audacity. Justin was my standard for all men.

He was there for me when I went through the Mormon temple for the first time. Afterward, when I started to freak out, he took me dancing at a club just so I could feel more like myself again. He spent Christmas with my family and me in New York City during the year I lived there. That holiday was particularly heavy. My youngest brother had been given special permission to leave drug rehab to spend the holidays with us, but in a moment none of us saw coming, he ran away. Instead of boarding the subway with us, he stayed on the platform as the train pulled away.

The panic and helplessness I felt in that moment were suffocating. For the next 48 hours, we were consumed with fear, not knowing where he was or if he was safe. Finally, he showed up on my doorstep in Brooklyn, looking worn but unharmed. Those two days had been grueling, filled with the kind of raw, gut-wrenching worry that never leaves you. Justin, as always, was right there with me, his presence a steadying force through the chaos.

He was there when I got married, he was there when Lucy was born, and he was there when Lucy died. He was one of only a handful of non-family members in the room when we said our final goodbyes. While I was lying in bed next to Lucy, Vic was on one side of the bed stroking her hair and holding one of my hands, and Justin was holding my other hand on the other side of the bed. He brought food to the hospital and fed the countless friends and family who came to support us.

He was classy and interesting and enjoyed the finer things in life. He sent me beautiful silk scarves while I was on my mission; he spoke French; he ran Salt Lake's number one restaurant, Cucina Toscana; he sang like George Michael. I loved his siblings and parents, and they loved me. And my family loved him. He was like a brother to all of us. He came to family dinners, went on family vacations with us, and it was not uncommon to be talking on the phone with him and have him tell me he needed to answer the other line because my mom or dad was calling.

Justin's gift for connecting with strangers was legendary. He had this way of drawing people in, learning their stories, and making them feel important. Paul Canaan, one of our good friends, used to joke that you couldn't take Justin anywhere without him turning a five-minute errand into an hours-long adventure because he'd talk to everyone—clerks, gas station attendants, strangers on the street. He loved people, and they loved him right back.

Justin's talent for connection was on full display when he became the emcee for the nonprofit A Good Grief, which Vic and I founded after Lucy passed away. His charisma and ability to connect with an audience—whether they were grieving, healing, or simply searching for meaning—made him the perfect person to host those events. He had this way of infusing every room with warmth, humor, and a sense of belonging, making everyone feel like they were part of something important. He didn't just speak to people—he made them feel known, like they mattered.

His last text to me, which I got while sitting in *Les Misérables* rehearsal—about three days before he died—was asking me how close to Kyiv, Ukraine my parents currently were (my parents lived in Moscow and Kyiv for over six years) because he had a friend filming a documentary there and his friend needed to get to a safe place. Justin had friends everywhere. I don't know a single person who met him who didn't love him.

He had his struggles. I think it is why he had such a tender heart. He knew the reality of pain. I will never forget the day he asked me to go to his house near Liberty Park. Lucy was about three months old. I sat in his messy living room (his house was being remodeled . . . but let's be honest, his house was always messy) while he stained the new cabinets in his kitchen. We chatted about some of his friends and their latest projects: photography and painting. And then he stopped what he was doing, knelt down at my feet, and told me he needed to tell me something. The tears flowed down his cheeks as he confided in me that he was gay. He was trembling. He explained how he had prayed, and he had fasted until he was 130 pounds (he's six feet tall), but nothing worked. He told me that if he could cut off one of his limbs and have God take away this struggle, he would gladly do it. Oh, how I wish we weren't raised in a religion that viewed his homosexuality as a sin!

I cried with him that day. I listened, and I hugged him and told him how much I loved him, just like he had done for me so many times before and continued to do until the day he died. Sometimes, Vic and I would sit in bed with the phone on speaker and talk to Justin about his heartaches. We'd also talk about business ideas; he had such a creative mind and was always starting new projects (we both had ADD, but I don't think either of us knew it). We always talked about traveling to France together one day. We'd talk about food and our families, church, music . . . there weren't many topics I can think of that we DIDN'T talk about.

No matter what was said, we were just saying "I love you" with every conversation. There were times he'd retreat into a dark, black hole and not want to come out. But eventually, he always did. He lived with his sister and her four children in their beautiful home in Bountiful. He loved his nieces and nephews immensely. He couldn't hide for long before a loved one would coax him out of his depression.

Justin was a builder. He built up everyone around him. He made you feel like the most special person in the room. It was truly his gift. If you go to his memorial facebook page and read what people have written about him, you will see that I am not exaggerating here. He was an absolutely beautiful soul.

Justin knew how to create magic with every person he met.

So when I say that I'm happy for him—happy that he is home—it is because I know about the wars that were raging in his heart. He often told me he just wanted to go home. He was so weary. He said he felt he lived a life of "almosts": I can *almost* be happy with a woman . . . but not quite. I can *almost* be happy with a man . . . but I struggle with the gay lifestyle and the guilt. I can *almost* be rich and famous (most of his friends were), but I just want to live with my family and serve people.

You know that Howard Jones song from the '80s?

> You can look at the menu, but you just can't eat
> You can feel the cushions, but you can't have a seat
> You can dip your foot in the pool, but you can't have a swim
> You can feel the punishment, but you can't commit the sin.
> (from "No One is to Blame")

He used to say that was his theme song.

Yes, he came close to taking his life at one point. But he was in a wonderful and happy spot when he passed away. He did not take his own life. He had just finished two intense weeks of parties and dinners at Sundance (including a birthday party for the actress Geena Davis) and was supposed to take over ownership of Cucina Toscana the day after he died. I firmly choose to believe that he truly wore himself out in the service of others. It was not uncommon for him to wear himself ragged. He would not eat at his incredible dinners; he was too busy serving and hosting. He'd go through the Wendy's drive-thru at 2 a.m. then go home and crash. In the days before he died, he was looking dehydrated.

The beautiful, powerful, vibrational energy of love he exuded is missing from this world. I can feel its absence. But it also matters that he left an incredible legacy and impression on those of us left behind.

I miss his gigantic laugh, the safety of his hug, the freedom he granted me to be myself—to call and talk about everything and nothing. To sob uncontrollably because motherhood is too hard, and death is too hard. To talk about marriage and business ideas and church and money.

Justin sang at my daughter's funeral. Six years later, I sang at his.

While his beautiful mother made her way down the corridor of the funeral hall where Justin's body would be throughout the service, she saw me awaiting the casket and fell into my arms, not having the strength to complete the final steps to her pew. I linked arms with her and bore the weight of some of her body and immeasurable grief while escorting her to her seat. She was surprised to see me—a fellow survivor—standing there with arms open, unafraid to witness the rawness of her sorrow. Seeing me upright—breathing, present—gave her permission to let go, to break open. In that moment, I knew that simply being there, standing with her, was enough.

I have felt Justin near me and even communicating with me since his death. I've even laughed with him. There have been a handful of times while listening to music in my car when I look over at the empty passenger's seat and know he's there. I feel incredibly grateful knowing he is with Lucy. I feel incredibly grateful that I was a small part of his life and he mine. I love you, Justin. Thank you for loving me and Vic so perfectly.

I know it is so cliche, but I want to do better at expressing my love and gratitude to everyone in my life. We never know how much time we have on earth together. And we never, ever know the depths of heartache people are experiencing.

So that's my Justin. My incredible, unforgettable, wonderful Justin. One of the best men I have ever known who taught me, among many things, that every stranger has a story.

The Power of "Momentary Magic"

One of the biggest perks of living in Park City is the easy access to world-class ski resorts. On the rare days when the stars align, I head to the resort while my kids are at school. Most often, I go solo.

I always bring my AirPods, squeezing them under my ski helmet so I can sing and "ski dance" my way down the mountain. Yes, I highly recommend it.

A few years ago, I pulled up to the Peak 5 chairlift, fully in the zone, hoping to ride the lift alone. There wasn't even a line. *YAS, KWEEN!*

I skied right up to the spot where the chair would swoop me up, ready for some peaceful, solo time. But just before the chair reached me, two snowboard dudes slid in on either side. *Stop the madness.* I wasn't in the mood to share a long lift ride with two stoner snowboarders.

Some days, I'm up for chatting on the lift. You know the drill: *Where are you from? How long are you in Park City? Yep, I live here. Yes, it's amazing. Yep, my kids are in school. I time it so precisely that I'm driving home behind their school bus. What do you do for work? Blah, blah, blah.* *Full disclosure: I've made a few genuine friends this way, but this was *not* one of those days.

To my chagrin, the dudes struck up a conversation. Did I aggressively double tap my AirPods to pause my music? Possibly. Picture me in a ski helmet and gloves, slapping the side of my face hard enough to make the AirPods work through all the layers. Very graceful.

Turns out, they were actually nice guys. I don't remember where they were from—California maybe—or what they did for work, but I'll never forget what one of them said just as we exited the chairlift.

Because they were so friendly and open, I thought, *What the hell?* I laid it all out—told them about my theater degree, how my daughter died, how I'm now a keynote speaker. I figured, *I'll never see them again. What's there to lose?*

They listened. Attentively (maybe that was the weed gummies). Their empathy and genuine responses were surprising and touching.

Then came the truth bomb.

One of them, with a smile, casually remarked, "Life really has a way of working out if we're willing to work with it."

Life has a way of working out—*if we're willing to work with it.*

If this were a text message, I'd insert the sobbing emoji right here.

That's the beauty of momentary magic—it teaches us to see the world differently. It invites us to open our hearts to the idea that every person we meet has something to offer, even if it's just for a moment. Justin lived this truth. His gift for connecting with strangers reminds me that in a world full of pain, joy can be found in the simplest interactions.

Every stranger has a story. Sometimes, those brief, magical moments of connection turn out to be the most important stories we're part of.

We are never truly alone as long as we're willing to reach out, to hold a hand, to bear witness. This is the legacy Justin leaves behind— the power of being present, of showing up, and of letting love, even for a fleeting moment, light the way.

From the very first time we met as perfect strangers, Justin embodied my dad's favorite quote (from one of my dad's old mentors): "There are two types of people in the world: those I love, and those I haven't met yet."

Justin taught me one of life's greatest lessons: the magic of brief but profound connections with strangers. He believed every encounter, no matter how fleeting, held the potential for connection. A smile, a conversation, a moment of shared understanding—these small gestures are what make us human. They remind us that we are never truly alone.

At Justin's funeral, his mother found solace in my arms, and I discovered an even deeper understanding of what it means to be present for someone. Life is full of these flashes of connection that, if we allow ourselves to be open to them, can transform us. Justin embodied that magic. He connected with everyone he met, leaving an imprint on their hearts.

Bringing "Momentary Magic" to a Professional Setting

Justin's ability to create meaningful connections from even fleeting moments holds invaluable lessons for the professional world. Whether interacting with clients, customers, or colleagues, brief but authentic engagement can foster trust and loyalty.

The secret to these quick connections often lies in two simple acts: offering a genuine compliment or asking thoughtful questions. In customer service, a kind word or a curious question can turn a routine interaction into a memorable experience. With clients, prioritizing connection over mere business solidifies relationships.

Even in the workplace, the smallest moments of connection—rooted in sincerity—can have lasting impact.

CHAPTER 18

The Power of Being a Witness

Healing Needs a Witness

I recently came across the idea that "healing needs a witness." But what does that really mean?

Amit Ray describes it beautifully: "Witnessing is the alchemy of enlightenment. It can transform mud into gold" (widely attributed, though original source is unknown). Being a compassionate observer to someone's life, or a particular moment of their suffering, is transformative for both the one in pain and the one bearing witness.

To bear witness is to say, "You are not alone. I see you. I honor your experience. Your pain matters to me. I hold you in my love." When someone silently, without judgment, witnesses your heartbreak—without trying to fix it, without flinching from the enormity of your grief—their presence holds profound power.

Healing begins when someone bears witness.

We all need someone to say, "I see you. I believe you. I acknowledge the depth of your pain and loss. No one should carry the weight of an untold story alone."

When we bear witness, we offer our attention and love without condition. And when we allow someone to bear witness to us, we give ourselves permission to be known, to be seen in our rawest form.

I am deeply grateful for those who have borne witness to my journey. I am especially grateful for my stalwart, brave, and faithful husband, Vic. He has been my greatest witness and cheerleader, standing by me with unwavering strength. But grief isn't a one-way street—we've had to take turns holding each other up, trading the burden of our heartbreak as we've navigated our loss together. Our love has been a lifeline, a shared witness to each other's deepest sorrows.

And beyond our personal circle, we've been lifted by the love of our church family and the countless Instagram followers who have followed our story for years. They've stood as faithful witnesses, offering their support, prayers, and kindness from near and far. Their presence, whether in person or through the digital realm, has been a steady source of strength.

Building the Bridge to Your Future Self

Healing is not a solitary endeavor. There is no meeting your future self, no hope for that future self, without being upheld by others. It is through connection—through the witnessing of our pain—that we begin to build a bridge toward who we can become.

I have never physically built a bridge, but I know the emotional and spiritual mechanics of it. On the day my daughter passed, part of me died with her. My old self was laid to rest, and the chasm between who I was and who I would become felt impossibly wide. Her loss was like a cruel magic trick—a vanishing act with no return.

But the persistent and hopeful humans around me, those who did not turn away from my despair, helped me start building that bridge. They pulled me out of the depths of my grief, not by offering answers but by sitting with me in the darkness. Their presence alone had healing power, and through their witnessing, they became the architects of my new self.

The Undervalued Power of Witnessing

The healing power of being a witness is often underestimated. Those of us who continue to rise, who place our feet on the ground each day and choose to live, are walking miracles. We are the soul contractors, showing others how to build a bridge back to themselves.

For a long time, you may feel like a stranger to yourself. The process of being rebuilt into something new is confusing, disorienting, and often unwelcome. But hold fast to those who have survived the storm—those who can see the sturdy ground on the other side. You may resist the rebuild; after all, you didn't ask for it. You no longer recognize the shape of your life, or even yourself.

But trust me when I say that your radiant, powerful future self is waiting for you. You can only meet her if you allow others to help you build the bridge. And one day, perhaps years or even decades from now, you will step onto that bridge—one built by hands and hearts that loved you when you couldn't love yourself—and meet her. You will embrace her with gentleness and grace, and together, you will step into a new realm of existence.

Putting the "Power of Witnessing" Into Practice in a Professional Setting

The act of being a witness in the workplace holds just as much power as it does in our personal lives. We often rush to offer solutions when a colleague or employee is struggling, but sometimes what people need most isn't an immediate fix but the knowledge that they are seen, heard, and valued.

Here's how you can practice being a witness in your professional environment.

- **Listen without interrupting**. When a coworker or employee opens up about a challenge, resist the urge to immediately offer advice or solutions. Instead, focus on truly hearing them. Let them finish their thoughts, and make space for silence if necessary.

- **Acknowledge their feelings**. Simple phrases like, "I can see how difficult this is for you," or "I understand that you're going through a lot" can go a long way in validating someone's experience. Acknowledgment is a powerful form of connection.

- **Offer presence, not perfection**. Sometimes, just being there—whether in person or virtually—can provide immense support. When a team member is overwhelmed, your calm, compassionate presence may be the witness they need to feel steadier on their feet.

- **Create a culture of nonjudgmental support**. Encourage an atmosphere where employees and colleagues feel safe to share their challenges without fear of judgment. When people trust that they'll be met with empathy instead of criticism, they're more likely to seek help and grow.

- **Model vulnerability**. By being willing to share your own struggles, you set an example for others. Let them see that it's OK to not have all the answers, and that it's human to lean on each other.

In a world where productivity and performance often take precedence, offering someone the gift of being seen in their struggle can be transformative. Whether it's during a team meeting, a one-on-one conversation, or a chance interaction in the break room, choosing to be a witness fosters deeper connections and builds trust. When people feel truly seen, they're more likely to bring their whole selves to work—and that's when the real magic happens.

CHAPTER 19

Carrying Lucy's Legacy, A Letter from Aunt Amy

Dear Lucy,

Wednesday was the day after your funeral. We'd been up late on Tuesday, after the beautiful service, watching videos of you. I tried to sleep that night, but I kept seeing you bouncing in that Johnny Jumper, eyes full of light, curls wrapping around your little head as you twisted and squealed. I kept hearing Molly, your mommy's, voice during those videos. Any mother knows the voice. It is the voice that can only come from a mother's mouth.

The voice is gentle, but delighted—seeing something in their child that only she can see. No matter how much you love someone else's child, even your sister's child, your voice will never sound like that. In the end, I suppose, it is the voice of wonder and admiration, both at your child, and at yourself for creating her.

After that sleepless night, I woke at 4:30 a.m. to shower and get to the airport. I struggled with my feelings, pained that I had to leave your mom in her time of greatest need and elated that I would be reunited with Jack, who I hadn't seen in almost ten days.

I also had another feeling, the unmistakable symptoms of the flu. As Chad, Uncle Nathan, Marie, and I loaded ourselves into the car in the darkness of the early morning, the birds in the mountains of Park City where your mom and dad live were already singing. I took one last look at their front porch, lovingly decorated with pink and purple bows and full to the brim with flowers of every kind, and we pulled away.

Because Nana and I had to fly to Utah so unexpectedly after hearing about your accident, we flew standby, thanks to the generosity of Nana's friend. That meant I was flying standby on the way home to Michigan as well.

I had great luck on the first leg. I got from Salt Lake to Phoenix on the first flight and I had an entire row to myself. I stretched out and slept, holding off my flu symptoms for the time being. I knew the next flight to Detroit was booked, but I prayed and prayed that I could get on. My flu was now in full swing; this flight would put me in Detroit within minutes of Chad's arrival, and it would give me time to try and sleep for the first time in three nights.

My heart soared when the amplified voice of the US Air desk agent called my name, the last of the standby passengers she called, and gave me a boarding pass. Sure, it was a middle seat, but I didn't care if they had to put me in the bathroom, I had a seat!

As soon as I'd settled in and called my mother-in-law, who had been watching Jack, to tell her the good news, a flight attendant came toward me, looking me straight in my eyes.

"I'm sorry," she said, "We are going to have to ask you to leave the plane. Someone with a ticket but without a seat assignment arrived late."

I started crying immediately. I tried to leave the plane, but people were still boarding, so I had to go to the back of the plane and wait for everyone to get on. I broke down. The flight attendants tried to console me with Diet Pepsi, but I was beyond consolation.

I finally left the plane, my entire body aching to hold Jack, and my heart aching even more thinking of your mom's longing to hold you again. I felt sorry for myself, I'll admit it.

I sat in a chair as the boarding area cleared, pulling myself together, but just barely. I saw a woman sitting in a wheelchair, alone, near the now closed boarding door. As I got up to stretch, I heard this woman ask if there was something to eat nearby. The employee, who was just getting off duty, basically dismissed her, explaining, "There may be something down this way, I'm not sure."

I hesitated, I'll admit. I think at another time in my life, before I felt weighed down with what I considered my own burdens, I would not have hesitated. I would have simply asked her what I could do to help. In fact, I distinctly remember helping a woman in an airport once when I was flying alone as a minor.

But that part of me, the part on constant lookout for how to help others, even, or especially, strangers, has been buried. Your death, and the subsequent outpouring of love (which seems an inadequate word for what I saw and heard), unearthed this feeling again. I went to this woman, Joyce, introduced myself, and asked her if I could go and get her something to eat. She was thrilled and my heart soared seeing her response.

Returning with her meal, we conversed briefly about hoping to get on the next flight to Detroit. I left to take a nap and saw her again as I approached the new departure gate. I lifted my crossed fingers in an "I hope we both get on this flight" signal. We sat in stunned silence as a seemingly unending crowd boarded the flight. Not a single standby passenger was called.

Now there was time for real conversation—the next flight to Detroit wasn't scheduled to leave for over six hours. She told me what she would be missing if she didn't make this flight: a commemoration of the death of her son 13 years ago who died at age 13. He was born with spina bifida, along with a host of other physical and mental disabilities. She spent 13 years of her life in the hospital caring for him.

She was so excited to share all the details with me about his funeral 13 years ago—how doctors who had cared for him flew in from around the world, how many tears and laughs were shared, all the bouquets of balloons that decorated the church. He knew death was coming, so he had it all planned out, right down to what he would wear. He told his mom he would "go out with a bang." She realized when he died, just after midnight, that it was Memorial Day and that many guns would be fired that day in honor of those who died. She said she laughed right out loud sitting there next to him. People thought she was crazy, but she found so much joy and comfort in that thought.

If she didn't make this flight she would miss this celebration of his life and commemoration of his passing!

We talked more. She told me about what she called "a few other struggles" she had: two strokes, caring for her mother with cancer who was still alive, her husband leaving her recently with no warning but a text message, her sister being murdered and leaving Joyce to raise her three children, and more.

I just listened and listened. There wasn't a note of self-pity in her voice, just an explanation of what her life had been like. At some point we stopped talking and I just looked at her and said, "Your life has been so full of grief. I hope you've had some joy."

With no hesitation, none whatsoever, she replied, "Oh, Amy. I've had more joy than I've had grief."

She must find joy in every day, in every breath, in every tree, in every person's eyes to tip the scales to the side of happiness after having so many struggles, that it was apparent that this was exactly what she did.

She took a few phone calls from her family in Detroit, desperate to know when she would arrive, and she told them about "the nice lady named Amy from Ann Arbor who is taking care of me."

I visited the airline desk a couple of times during the six plus hours, and I knew that I was much higher on the standby list than Joyce was. The final flight of the day, set to arrive at 1:30 a.m. Detroit time, was her only hope to be part of this celebration.

I made up my mind, though it wasn't easy, that I would give up my seat for her if it came to that. I was still sick, still tired, still full of a strange mix of sorrow and happiness, but I felt so peaceful about it.

134

When the flight began to board, they called my name. I told them that I would wait to board until I knew Joyce's status. I waited and waited. I didn't want to stay the night in Phoenix, don't get me wrong, but I knew that it was what I was supposed to do. What your accident taught me. What love would do.

At the last minute, they called her name and we yelled out in joy! We walked on the plane together (well, technically, I pushed her on the plane). I talked the flight attendant into upgrading her to first class since there was an empty seat there (the only one on the plane). Otherwise, she'd have to hobble herself all the way to the back row without the help of her wheelchair.

Thank you, Lucy. My life has changed because of you. It isn't this experience that is necessarily important, but the change that it represents.

I have so far to go, but I'll get there. Thank you again, Lucy. I love you.

Aunt Amy

Amy's letter to Lucy invites us to reflect on the power of love, connection, and quiet strength of bearing witness to others' pain. In helping a stranger, Joyce, on what could have been an exhausting and frustrating day, Amy reminds us of Lucy's legacy—one of selflessness, empathy, and healing through connection.

When you see someone, truly see them, and bear witness to their struggles without judgment or expectation, you open the door to transformation. Just as Amy reached out to Joyce, you, too, have the capacity to reach beyond your own sorrow and lift someone else. Healing comes not only from being seen but also from seeing others.

When we share our grief and pain, we also create an opportunity for profound change. In extending yourself, even while hurting, to someone else who is suffering, you create a ripple of compassion that brings light to both sides. This is Lucy's gift—a reminder that love, connection, and witnessing the lives of others are some of the greatest acts of healing you can offer.

Lucy's legacy lives on in every act of generosity and in the hearts of those who choose to live with more love, more connection, and more joy, even in the face of immense sorrow. The invitation is open to you now—will you choose to bear witness to someone else's pain, just as Amy did? Will you create moments of connection that allow healing to flourish? Lucy's short life shows that these small, powerful acts are what matter most.

In Vic's words:

> More often than not in life, we don't know the effects we have on the lives of others; how the things we do, small or big, ripple down through time and generations; how what we do changes what others perceive and how they will chart their course through life.

> Lucy was "just a two-year-old"—a beautiful, fully silly, sometimes ornery and petulant but sweet two-year-old. And yet, even before her departure, she forced a new perspective of life and the world on me. She forever altered and changed me and the course of my life. She didn't do anything particularly grand or epic other than love life, love her mom, love others, and love me. I guess she provided me with a glimpse of just how happy I will someday be. It is nice to catch a glimpse every once in a while.

CHAPTER 20

In the Wake
of Love and Loss

Since Lucy died, life has continued to evolve in ways both beautiful and heartbreaking. We were blessed with two more children—our daughter Zoë and our son, Peter. His name carries deep meaning for us, as we chose it after two iconic Peters: Peter Pan, a symbol of endless youth and adventure, and Peter, the High King of Narnia, from C.S. Lewis's *The Chronicles of Narnia*. Those books held a special place in our hearts long before Lucy was born. During my pregnancy with her, Vic would read *The Chronicles of Narnia* to me at night to help me fall asleep. It was there, in the magical world of Narnia, that we fell in love with the name Lucy.

Zoë came into our lives in her own extraordinary way. She was due on Lucy's birthday, but in true Zoë fashion, she decided to arrive five days early, bringing with her a vibrant head of red hair and a spirit all her own. Her name means *life*, and she has been a living reminder of hope and resilience in our lives.

It seemed only fitting that Lucy's headstone should carry a line from *The Chronicles of Narnia*—a quote that perfectly captures the fleeting beauty of her time with us:

"I do love that tune. But really, I must go home. I only meant to stay for a few minutes."

Lucy's presence in our lives, though brief, left a mark that will echo for generations.

Peter and Zoë have grown up surrounded by Lucy's story, a legacy woven into the fabric of their family long before they were born. They've heard the stories, seen the pictures, and felt the silent weight their parents carry—the unspoken heartache that hovers in the background of everyday life. They've come to understand, in their own gentle ways, the impact of an older sister they never had the chance to meet. From a young age, they learned that love and loss can coexist, that there is beauty in remembering, and that honoring Lucy is part of what makes their family whole.

Each year, we visit the cemetery together. Peter often goes reluctantly, the sadness of it sitting heavily on his heart. He's told us it makes him feel something he can't quite name yet, a feeling too big for his young years. And yet, he comes along, his quiet presence a small tribute to his sister, a gesture of love in its own way. Zoë, with her boundless spirit, brings her own light to these visits. She'll hold my hand, ask questions, and fill the quiet with her sweetness, somehow sensing how these moments are sacred. Both of them, in their own ways, have accepted these rituals, learning that honoring someone's life can be as simple as showing up, as powerful as being present.

At school and with friends, they find ways to talk about her, sometimes surprising us with their wisdom. She's not just a figure of the past to them—she's woven into their lives, remembered in bedtime prayers and conversations. Through their connection to Lucy, they've become tender and kind, their hearts more open to the pain and joy in the world around them. They understand, perhaps more deeply than most, that life is precious, that people matter, and that love doesn't end, even in the face of loss. In the way they carry Lucy's story, Peter and Zoë honor her every day, allowing her legacy to shape the goodness and grace they bring into the world.

In watching them embrace their sister's memory, my deepest hope is that Peter and Zoë will grow up to see relationships and connections as life's true treasures. I hope they'll understand that it's not the length of time we have with someone but the depth of the bond that matters most. Through Lucy's legacy, I want them to feel that the love we give and the compassion we show are what endure. If they carry one lesson forward, I hope it's this: that connection is what makes us whole, and that it's the most precious thing we'll ever have.

There is a strange kind of letting go that comes with living through and surviving one of the worst all-consuming nightmares a human can endure. It's not a resignation but a liberation. When you lose everything, the clutter of life falls away, and it becomes painfully, beautifully clear what truly matters. And for us, that has been the incredible wealth we've found in the commodity of connection.

I often joke that, in a place like Park City, we are the "everyday millionaires" because, unlike most people in town, we don't drive a Tesla (though our kids thought our Toyota minivan was one—so close!). But despite what we drive or how glamorous—or not—our daily routines may be, we are wealthy beyond measure in what truly counts.

When you stand at the edge of the abyss, stripped of all illusions of control, you realize that the only thing that holds you together—truly, the only thing—is love. It's the connections you nurture, the relationships you invest in, the community that stands by you when everything else falls apart. We are wealthy beyond measure because we have chosen to build a life filled with deep, meaningful connection.

Our lives today are richer because of this clarity. The friends who held us when we couldn't stand, the strangers who reached out with kindness, the family who stood, unwavering, by our side—these connections are our true fortune. The pain we have endured has given us a greater capacity for love, for empathy, for understanding the depths of the human heart. And because of that, we are able to live fully, love deeply, and find meaning even in the darkest of days.

Lucy's life, short as it was, showed us what truly matters. And in her absence, we've learned how to build a life around that knowledge. We are not defined by the loss of our daughter but by the love that continues to flow through us because of her.

www.ingramcontent.com/pod-product-compliance
Lightning Source LLC
Chambersburg PA
CBHW061806120626
46550CB00005B/2154